God's Way and Family

The Biblical Definition of Family, the Benefits of Being a Family of God and More!

AUDREY L. DICKEY, PH.D.

Kingdom Advance Publishing
P. O. Box 48288
Los Angeles, California 90048
877.333.5075

robertandaudreydickeyministries.org

Printed in the United States of America

ISBN: 978-0-9997611-4-4

Library of Congress Control Number: 2017919835
Kingdom Advance Publishing, Los Angeles, CA

Christian Life / Family

DEDICATION

Friends come and friends go but family should be forever!

To my siblings: Harold, Deborah, Sharon, Belinda, Michael, Lynn, Jacqueline, Glenna and Sean. Thank you for your impartation into my life and for all the wonderful memories of our childhood and adult life we share.

I also thank my brothers and sisters for their love and patience over the years as my immediate family sojourned on this extraordinary journey to take hold of our destiny.

CONTENTS

INTRODUCTION

Anyone who is familiar with me can attest I am not interested in the *opinions* of people, male or female, not even my own, when in conflict with the Word of God. We all have opinions, but are we able to truly backup what "we think" and what "we feel?" For thoughts and feelings come and go!

There is but one standard that will remain intact and that is the Word of God, God's Holy Bible. I read both the Old Testament and the New Testament. The Old Covenant conceals mysteries that are revealed in the New Covenant.

Furthermore, the Word of God says in 2 Timothy 3:16 that, "Every Scripture is God-breathed (given by His inspiration) and profitable for instruction, for reproof *and* conviction of sin, for correction of error *and* discipline in obedience, [and] for training in righteousness…"

I also enjoy reading and studying from other materials as I am directed by Holy Spirit. As I am sensitive to the Father's heart I am able to receive by yielding to His way and not to my own. Like most, that have a relationship with God are able to do.

God's heart reveals that He loves people and He loves families. He feels strongly about this and has declared what a family is. A point that is made in this resource. Which includes the benefits and rewards He has for the family.

Furthermore, there is a type of people that God calls 'His own' family. Those members that were born into God's family and those who were grafted into His family by adoption and are therefore born-again.

However, those that were born into the family will need salvation the same as those who were grafted in if they are to experience the New Covenant and to receive eternal life.

We all must come in faith, believing the Father's (Elohim; YHVH) heart was to have a people who chose to love Him and receive Him as their own, a part of their family; simply because He chose to love them and receive them *first* as a part of His.

As we respect the Lord's heart and receive His love for us, there is no limit to what He will do. We have entered into a new time in history where God is pouring out His Spirit which will demonstrate His Glory, His tangible *presence* into our midst in a way that has never happened or been seen before.

God is raising up His family to be stronger than ever. His family can comprise anyone in the world, Jew or Gentile (secular, the nations) who chooses Him and chooses His way of doing things.

What God sanctions as a family is designed to train up and produce those of godly character. Each family member will be anointed by God to cause positive change that will affect generations to come.

We will define biblical roles within the family unit that will restore order and place integrity back into the home. Things are possible if family members are willing to set their priorities to do things according to God's way.

Moreover, in this resource, we will touch on the different aspects and types of natural families (biological, blended, single, adopted, and so forth). At the same time, we will explore the godly or spiritual family and how they play a significant part in the overall role of a family today.

Chapter 1

What is a Family, its Purpose and the Qualities that Make it Strong?

"In the beginning [before all time] was the Word (Christ), and the Word was with God, and the Word was God Himself. He was present originally with God. *All things were made and came into existence through Him*; and without Him was not even one thing made that has come into being" John 1:1-3.

In Genesis 2:7 it tells us **God created the first family** by forming mankind from the dust of the ground and breathing into his nostrils the breath or Spirit of life. And thereafter this new creation which consisted of a "male and female" became a living being, Genesis 1:26; Colossians 3:10.

God then performed surgery, removing a part of his side (a rib) from the male body which was already equipped with the female at the time He created the male. The female needed to be formed which took place when God *built-up and made* the wo-man for Adam with the part of his body that was removed.

This female partner was to be with him for the rest of his life. **This would be the beginning and foundation of the family** as we know it on earth. A Child-Free Family until the birth of their first son.

The Bible Verifies this in Genesis 2:21-23,

> And the Lord God caused a deep sleep to fall upon Adam; and while he slept, He took one of his ribs *or* a part of his side and closed up the [place with] flesh. And the rib *or* part of his side which the Lord God had taken from the man *He built up and made into a woman, and He brought her to the man.* Then Adam said, This [creature] is now bone of my bones and flesh of my flesh; she shall be called Woman, because she was taken out of a man.

He who created them from the beginning made them male and female to be joined in marriage. And God said, "For this reason a man shall leave his father and mother and shall be united firmly (joined inseparably) to his wife, and the two shall become one flesh? So they are no longer two, but one flesh..." Matthew 19:4-6.

The very foundation of a family is the marriage. The foundation of the marriage will determine the strength of the family. When the marriage begins with a male and female who are both "whole" that in itself will be the foundation to build upon.

When these two individuals, who have supernaturally become one at the time of their marriage, come into the union with a sound mind (the mind of Christ, Phil. 2:5; 2 Tim. 1:7), secure in themselves, with goals and dreams, knowing who they are in Christ, filled with joy, expectation and hopeful towards building a wonderful life together, this is all that is necessary to have a vast and grand beginning.

As they continue growing in the same direction they will maintain and be steady as they become one (like-minded). Together they are in a position to seek God for the purpose of their marriage. What is it they are to accomplish together or as a family that may need intervention from Almighty God?

Also, another component that will carry their family is their love for God, their love for each other and a healthy love for themselves as valued human beings and contributors to their family unit.

Coming together with the right perspective, practicing humility, knowing they won't be able to achieve their dreams and goals on their own, in their own strength. This will open the door even wider for God to be *their Source* and *the Light* will show them the way. *A Door* will open and they will be able to receive the proper help from their "Helper" – Holy Spirit! John 16: 7. Their journey can be exciting if they have the right perspective.

By placing their family in God's hands, truly trusting Him with the blessing He gave them, God will manifest His wisdom, strength and glory. As long as He is at the forefront God will continue to impart and cause them to have a blessed and strong family.

The family/mishpochah (in Hebrew) is the strongest institution in the world not only because it was created and built by Almighty God but because He is in covenant with their foundation. Without the marital tie the family circle, family institution and parental love and care would have been altogether unknown.

Proverbs 24:3-4 tells us,

> Through skillful *and* godly Wisdom is a house (a life, a home, a family) built, and by understanding it is established [on a sound and good foundation], And by knowledge shall its chambers [of every area] be filled with all precious and pleasant riches.

This scripture clearly outlines the intent God had for the family was for them to walk and **live with *godly* wisdom** for their lives and families. *He said the family is established on a sound and good foundation which is the Word of God.* Knowledge (divine revelation) will cause their home to increase and be filled with precious and pleasant riches. Rich in love, rich in God's presence, rich in good relationships, rich in the anointing, rich in health, rich in wealth, rich in good strategies for business, rich in success, *and rich in every area of its chambers (home) which shall be filled with precious and pleasant riches.*

"Joy is a distinctive quality of biblical faith in the Old and New Testaments. Joy was intended to be shared whether in worship or in family togetherness. Because of the relationship with Christ the Christian family amplifies joy which is a fruit and characteristic of the Holy Spirit who was given to guide the family. Therefore, *uniting the family in Christian faith results in joy for the family*, Acts 16:34. Happy experiences can be shared in joy.

Joy is a gift from God. Joyful experiences shared by the family create memories that continue through life. Families need to guard against letting the difficulties of daily tasks rob them of time to plan enjoyable experiences together," [1] John 15:13-15.

The family relationship *instituted by God is the very foundation of all human societies* as well as it occupies a prominent place throughout the holy scriptures. The germ or source and representation of every fellowship known to mankind came through a family.

"When the atmosphere of the home and the parent's attitude is good plus the marriage is secure, then that family is a core or base where a person's character is formed, integrity is born, values we live by are made clear, goals are set and attitudes are formed that last a life time" as so well stated by Dr. Billy Graham (paraphrased).

A body of people living together such as roommates, friends, fraternities, sororities, college dormitories, sport teams, convents, military personnel, firemen, gangs and similar groups may refer to themselves *"as a family"* and they may even have some of the same functions, traditions, develop soul ties and become best of friends really caring and loving one another but **they are not who God has sanctioned as a "family."**

A family does not exist merely to fill a void of loneliness, share expenses, experiences, work or even house rules. If this is not enough proof know even people in the world (non-Believers) know the difference. For instance, if someone became ill and a family member had to provide family history, or insurance documents, or be allowed in the intensive care unit of a hospital what is the probability of a close friend having this information or even be allowed in?

Even if they had the information what is the possibility of them having the authority to make decisions about a non-family member's wellbeing? It is almost nil because one of the first questions asked is are you a member of the family, are you related?

Who God sanctions or approves of as a family in addition to who He refers to as the "True Family" is designed to train up and produce people with godly character that will function for the Kingdom of God within their given society. A family is to bring into place a unit of individuals with like thinking and shared godly morals. In addition, each family member is anointed by God to cause positive change that will affect generations to come. This is why the Lord places

emphasis on training up a child in the way they should go, Prov. 22:6.

I might add even though they may have disagreements among themselves basically no one else from outside of that family unit will have the same privilege.

Core values help discover each person's sense of self and to develop his identity. It is the family that is considered to be the essential *building block of any nation;* one reason being is *the family is focused on creating benefits for the next generation.* Therefore, a community is then formed from strong families thus growing into a city which then produces a society of people.

Genesis 14:14 NIV [2] is an Example of a Biblical Household During Ancient Times,

The household in biblical times included the primary family, servants and other family members and persons entrusted with various responsibilities for maintaining the household. Thus, in the household of Abram, children of servants were educated as soldiers from their youth. ***Education is a basic task of the household***. The wisdom literature of the Old Testament is particularly focused in the nurture and education of children in the household. (Emphasis added.)

According to Christian Authors the following Components are Qualities Necessary to have for a Strong Household

- Commitment, Communication, Acceptance, Adjustment, Respect, Responsibility, Empathy, Encouragement, Forgiveness, Sacrifice, Quality time and a Sense of Humor

These components are necessary to have a healthy and balanced marriage in your household and when both partners have these qualities first for their marriage and second for their family they will have the beginning stages of a healthy family structure.

I have elaborated on a few of the qualities listed above from *Marriage & Family, A Christian Journal of the American Association of Christian Counselors* and what it briefly says about commitment, communication and respect:

> ***Commitment*** *– is an unconditional promise, a pledge to a permanent union.* It is not a contract that requires reciprocal action by the partner but a covenant enacted without reservation. *A prenuptial agreement has no place in a Christian union or covenant.* It only prepares one's mind for a breakup later in the marriage. So, in essence you are preparing and expecting to fail at

marriage. What you expect is by faith what you will have. Therefore, ultimately you will have what you believe.

Communication – is shared meaning, occurring both verbally and non-verbally. *Only through open communication can effective decision-making, problem solving and conflict resolution occur.* Listening attentively facilitates understanding and earns the privilege to speak. Talking is more than the words uttered – the message greatly influenced by the tone and style of expression.

Respect – is to hold in high regard or esteem. It does not require agreement with or acceptance of opinion. *It does demand courtesy and politeness at all times*, Ephesians 5:33 and I Peter 3:7.

These are just a few of the instructions found in the Word of God to benefit a household. *The faithful application of biblical principles can bring new life and vitality to any household* no matter what stage the family is in, whether it be a household in strife, full of rebellious children, an unfaithful spouse and so forth. When we yield to build a healthy and strong marriage based on God's principles and commands we acquire the wisdom of God to carry it through and allow it to be the example for the family unit it needs to be.

Building on a Solid Foundation, Luke 6:46-49 NLT,

> So why do you keep calling Me 'Lord, Lord!' when you don't do what I say? I will show you what it's like when someone comes to Me, listens to My teaching, and then follows it. It is like a person building a house who digs deep and lays the foundation on solid rock. When the floodwaters rise and break against that house, it stands firm because it is well built. But anyone who hears and doesn't obey is like a person who builds a house without a foundation. When the floods sweep down against that house, it will collapse into a heap of ruins.

Additional Qualities, Attributes and Principles that are Taught and/or Found in a Healthy and Strong Family

1. A relationship with God which starts with salvation. The Word of God is taught to each member of the family
2. God's order within your home; A place of security and protection
3. Respect for one another and the younger respect their elders
4. An understand delegated authority
5. Our trust in God makes it easier to trust each other

6. Cohesiveness – having a closeness within the family unit, quality time
7. The family will preserve you; it is a place where you learn you are loved and have the freedom to be yourself
8. The family will provide you with your identity and sense of importance and acceptance. There won't be a need for a counterfeit family such as a gang and so forth
9. Family teaches you about morality; developing normally over the years as you process through different age groups. It teaches you can be different and enjoy your life
10. Adaptability – to be able to make changes and be flexible
11. Communication skills are taught in the family; how to listen, how not to be rude and interrupt; how to speak effectively
12. Empathy – think and feel as the other person; new perspective
13. Commitment - integrity, soundness, honesty and keeping your word
14. Creative use of Conflict - searching your heart and motive before confronting
15. Affirmation - affirming one another; respect and trust; asserting positively
16. Role Modeling - having good role models and examples in the home; family teach you self-worth and how to

build confidence and keep your emotions in check

17. Play and Leisure Time – balance in one's life and individual time is important; teaches time management

18. Discipline and Responsibility – maturity and strength; taking ownership, these things are learned within the family

19. Self-Respect - love yourself in a healthy way so you can love others. Take care of your health, appearance and do things for yourself without becoming self-centered and selfish

20. Family can teach you how to have balance, how to take care of your health and how to eat properly

21. Traditions - foundations, godly beliefs passed from generation to generation. Stable environment for the family

22. A Sense of Family History - roots, know your strengths and challenges

23. Teaches you humility. A willingness to be humble enough to seek and ask God and others for help in a time of crisis; Help others who cannot do anything for you

24. Family teaches members how to be civil with one another; how to socialize; how to share, to work together, listen, be considerate and how to have constructive arguments and problem solving

25. Extended family ties in your life are important too
26. Godly friends outside of the family; divine friendships
27. An understanding of managing finances using godly principles
28. Community Involvement – involved with some aspect of your society. Society is only as strong as its families. The family preserves society. The society is the reflection of the condition of the family
29. Political or Government Commitment – God requires we pray and vote for godly leaders. God placed families above government, work and so forth. Families determine the condition of its nation

The following *Elaborates* on some of the Qualities, Attributes and Principles that are Found in a Healthy and Strong Family

1. A Relationship with God – can begin through salvation with each individual family member, John 3:3, 7. At the age of accountability (somewhere around the age of twelve even though some children receive the Lord at an earlier age), have your children been introduced to the Lord in order to have an opportunity to receive Jesus Christ the Anointed One and Messiah as their Lord and Savior according to Romans 10:9?

Are the parents saved and serving God in the area He called them to, in which the person is equipped and anointed to serve God. Are they committed regardless of what their purpose or assignment in life is? Whether it is a minister, a businessman or businesswoman, a homemaker, an entrepreneur, a blue-collar worker, an entertainer, a sports figure or whatever your calling is. God has purposed a specific assignment for each and every person's life and a personal relationship with Him will cause them to fulfill their destiny and be successful.

Strong biblical families encourage the spiritual development of their members preferably bringing their children up in the Word of God. The Bible says to, "train up a child in the way he should go, and when he is old he will not depart from it," Proverbs 22:6. It further says, "All your children shall be taught by the Lord, and great shall be the peace (wholeness) of your children," Isaiah 54:13. Part of bringing them up in the Word of God is taking them to a good *Bible Teaching Word Church* that believes in the *Gifts of the Spirit* and receives all the promises of God. Seek God as a married couple or with your family and pray about which house of God should be your church home, (Gifts of the Spirit: I Cor.12:7-11; Eph. 4:11-12; Romans 12:6-15 and Romans 11:29).

"Many families have their own ethical standards" such as reverence for life, morals, setting good examples and role models for one another and their children. Godly principles will work for whoever puts them into motion. Ethical standards will give wise guidelines, hope, stability, morals and sound direction to help mold a person for the better. By having peace and understanding about many things in life, these principles can become a part of their lifestyle making it possible to live a blessed life.

However, the **"Biblical principles, rules and guidelines** *from the Word of God have been set in place by God to use in the home as The Standard."* With the benefit of *Salvation* these biblical principles, rules and guidelines from the Holy Scriptures will give each Born-again member of the family the authority, power (grace) and right to exercise the principles in the Word of God and receive the benefits to its fullest extent. Please realize principles, morals, rules, laws, guidelines, and standards *alone without Salvation* can never offer eternal life nor all that comes with having Salvation to function in the Kingdom of God while here on earth.

Our Lord and Savior has a plan for our lives, Jeremiah 29:11. His plan involves living a life of peace, joy, abundance, fullness, wholeness and victory with the fruit of the Spirit, Gal. 5:22-23. God is interested in our family being whole and complete wholeness is in Salvation.

Functioning with godly principles but *without Salvation* can be compared to *functioning in self-righteousness which is righteousness without power and being full of self and pride.* Believing because you are doing the "right" things, you are entitled to all God has promised, forgetting that a dear "price" was paid for the Righteousness that comes with Salvation.

In addition to eternal life, Salvation also gives godly authority, power, favor, mercy, protection, provision, deliverance, prosperity, promises fulfilled, health, peace of mind, godly relationships and many more blessings. This cannot be earned by any person; therefore, Salvation was given as a gift to be taken by faith through the grace of God.

Only then after receiving Jesus and studying His Word, learning of Him and His ways will a person not be moved by every doctrine that comes across their path. Furthermore, they will not have to be blown like a wave on the sea, driven and tossed by the wind for it says, "a double minded man is unstable in all his ways," James 1:6-8 KJV. (See *God's Way and Knowing the King* for additional details.)

2. Cohesiveness - Cohesion is an emotional bonding that family members have towards one another. It is more than just time together. Members feel close when they are together and not lonely and disconnected. They feel bonded but not "stuck together" but because they chose to "stick together" they have a sense of unity without a loss of individuality; and is a coalition that performs expected functions without interference. Honesty, listening, openness, verbal affection, sensitivity, supportiveness are a part of the closeness felt between family members who have healthy emotional bonds.

Also, spending time together is necessary to develop adequate communication and to build cohesion. **Family traditions require family time.** Children and spouses learn they are appreciated, valued, and have self-worth when other members spend time with them. The modeling and teaching parents provide for their children requires shared time, as does showing support to family members by attending school events and other occasions of special significance in the lives of family members.

Time taken to play and relax with our loved ones pays off in ways that keeping work caught up or the house completely in order never can. When we are realistic we see that the paper work never ends and there will always be something to do in the home, but our children and our mates will never again be as they are right now. If we don't take the time now to enjoy our families, we lose opportunity for memories and family togetherness. Some parents have lost years and now live with regrets that they missed so much of family time trying to make a living.

Healthy families know this and give play and leisure time priority. Note, if you are a family that did not have a lot of time together while the children were growing up, know that God is a God that redeems time, a God of restoration and He will give back to you and your family that which was stolen by the enemy, all you need to do is ask!

3.   Adaptability – Healthy families continually change and adapt as they grow through the life cycle. They have the ability to change in response to situational and developmental stress (children becoming adolescents, a wife becoming employed, a family member becoming ill or a sudden death, love ones losing their way or backsliding, husband suddenly unemployed and so on).

There will always be changes in families that will need attention and require members to adapt. Changes which cause the family to focus or adapt can affect individual members of the family who have to participate in the adjusting to what another member is going through if it is something that will affect the entire household. Some essentials to help adapt to these changes are: (1) reading the Word of God and acting on His Word; (2) having good leadership for guidance and direction to aid with family decision making. Good leadership is having the head of the family who is listening to and obeying God and is open to receive input from other members of the family but most importantly respecting the input (godly wisdom) from their spouse.

Keeping in mind when input is expressed, a healthy family member's request and feelings are without fear and intimidation. A healthy family will allow for individual self-confidence and self-expression as contributions are made towards decisions and directions for the family.

4. Discipline and Responsibility - Is definitely a part of family structure, it helps to set limits and create the framework for desired family behavior. The Word of God says, to "Train up a child in the way he should go [and in keeping with his individual gift or bent], and when he is old he will not depart from it." To train up is to take the responsibility of training, teaching and disciplining your child in the knowledge, understanding and wisdom of God which will empower them to discern and make wise choices in life. As we know, one wrong choice can ruin years of a person's life regardless of their age.

Discipline also demonstrates the love you have for your children by taking the time to care enough to correct their ways or actions in a firm but loving way. It sets boundaries for them and gives them a sense of security. Discipline for children is done on an individual basis because each child requires different action to be taken at various times. Why? Because they are individuals, each situation is to be dealt with according to what is appropriate for that particular child.

5. Communication Skills – Our tone of voice, body language, eye contact, silence, a touch, a hug or a gift are all forms of communication. In strong families' communication usually is direct and often. They have much to share and they enjoy sharing. They trust one another and are good listeners. When family members have truly been heard – not just the words, but their feelings acknowledged, they feel and sense a respect and appreciation because of the attention and empathy of the listener.

In communicating rules or guidelines for the home for example, strong healthy families discuss them along with the reasons for them. Rules should never be hidden or changed without acknowledgement from each family member. In our family we called rules "guidelines." We realized the word "rules" is used a lot in schools, with sports and in different places. The word rules can be a very "negative" word and seen as rigid and will automatically turn some people off when they hear the word, therefore, to receive cooperation from the entire family, guidelines or another similar word could be a better choice.

During conflict, strong healthy families seem to have the ability to keep their communication open and to be able to stay focused on the issues rather than on the person or persons with whom they are speaking.

Forgiveness is one of God's major tools to keep communication lines open. It is a decision we make and it is not based on how we feel. Many times, as we *choose* to forgive we can see and hear beyond the person or persons we are having conflict with and realize they may be reaching out for help. Many times, people are hurting, or are in some kind of bondage and/or fear that is preventing them from being able to communicate effectively or openly.

If we would just *choose to forgive*, take our focus off of the person or what was done and pray, then God would be in a position to intervene in the situation by giving us wisdom, direction, guidance, healing and miracles as needed to aid all parties involved in the conflict. When we ask for help He is faithful to answer and we must be faithful to receive and act.

6.   Commitment – When an individual is committed to his or her family, motivation is high to solve problems and to deal with conditions that threaten the family. *When families become busy and fragmented, those with high levels of commitment take the initiative to review the family's priorities and activities.* They proceed to make changes that will relieve the problem and/or condition that threatens the family. The members deliberately work together to set priorities for the use of family time. Commitment involves the promotion of the growth of other family members. Family members are concerned for one another's happiness and well-being. Commitment involves working on behalf of one's family and wanting the best for each other. It is not about anyone being self-centered but a family member's feeling he or she is a part of something larger than themselves.

If the members of your family have received their salvation then they should be committed to the ways of God as it is written in His Word, which is a process and it entails the renewing of the mind, Romans 12:2. If they are committed to God and His ways then they will be committed and faithful in everyday life going about doing good (what is right, decent and in order). They will keep their lives in tack by guarding what they watch, hear and say as much as possible and asking the Holy Spirit to help them accomplish this.

When committed they will also be led to pray for the family on a daily basis especially for those who do not know the Lord. They will be accessible to others in the family; they will strive to avoid taking anyone in the family for granted and instead will think of creative or possible ways to bless the family as a whole or individuals within it. They won't mind examining their actions and attitudes toward other family members and are willing to make any necessary adjustments so love can be expressed. *Last but not least, they will realize they will reap what they have invested in their family.*

7. Affirmation, Respect and Trust – For most of us the phrase we like best is "I love you." It can go a long way toward soothing a hurt, drying a tear, restoring a crumbling sense of self-worth, and maintaining a feeling of satisfaction and well-being when spoken with sincerity from the heart. *Supporting others in our family by letting them know we're interested in their projects, problems, feelings, opinions and being supportive and affirmed in return is essential to family health.*

We must learn to give respect for a family member's uniqueness and differences, even if we may not necessarily understand or agree with him or her. *Criticism, ridicule, and rejection* undermine self-esteem and severely restrict individual growth. In addition to exhibiting respect for others, a healthy family member should also insist on being respected in return.

Children in healthy families are allowed to earn trust as deemed appropriate by their parents. Children who know they are trusted are then able to develop self- confidence and a sense of responsibility for themselves and others.

It is equally important for parents to be realistic in their promises to children and honest about their own mistakes and shortcomings. Parents are to be willing and open to ask one another for forgiveness or to be able to apologize. It is important for parents to ask their children for forgiveness when they have made a mistake, misjudged someone or something. It is called practicing what you preach.

It is also important for children to see their parents trust and love each other. A loving relationship between parents breeds security in the children, and in turn fosters the ability to take risks to reach out to others, to search for their own answers, become independent, and develop a good self-image. The more children observe their elders in situations that demonstrate mutual trust, respect, and care, the more they are encouraged to incorporate these successful and satisfying behaviors into their own lives.

8. Traditions – Especially those traditions rooted in our cultural background help give us a sense of who we are as a family and as a community. Through tradition families find a link to the past and, consequently, a hope for the future.

Most successful families have someone who maintains and transmits the family story. They have traditions that help them keep alive their identity as a family. The traditions may vary greatly, from elaborate holiday celebrations to daily or weekly routines.

Traditions, special practices, customs and techniques unique to the family whether they are ways of celebrating birthdays or just having dinner together imprint their family identity in the hearts and memories of its members. Blended families may benefit particularly from the creation of new traditions which can generate a feeling of closeness and provide fuel for weathering the more difficult times. (See *God's Way and the Blended Family* for additional ways for successfully blending a family.)

9. An Understanding of Delegated Authority - Bottom line, if we place God before our family, then follow the order of God and listen to the delegated authorities God has placed in our lives, whether it be a parent, an employer, a state official, a teacher, a church leader or whomever it is in authority over us at the time. *When we render respect towards that person and follow the leading of the Holy Spirit we will experience a supernatural strength*, love and divine wisdom for our obedience. This will help us to maintain and have a joyful victorious family lifestyle.

10.   Biblical Economics - Is another major area required in order for a family to be healthy and strong. How a couple manages their finances is extremely important since most marriages fail as a result of poor management of the family income(s). Marriage is _between a husband, a wife and God,_ therefore, all that concerns the couple is also a concern to God. His principles when applied to their finances will assist tremendously in having the wisdom needed for management.

Once a couple realizes everything belongs to God and He makes them trustees of His possessions, it will be easier to operate within His economic system. They will understand they are stewards (they are His partners who manage what He has entrusted to them). This knowledge makes it easier to come in agreement with Deuteronomy 8:18 and Malachi 3:6-12 and other instructions the Lord has designated for their finances in order to increase their family financially. (See _God's Way and Finances_ for additional information regarding the handling of money.)

Chapter 2

The Different Types of Families that Shape and Develop Society

In our society we tend to think the *"True Family"* is the Nuclear or Biological Family or even the Traditional Nuclear Family. *The Nuclear Family* is a family that consists of a father, a mother and their biological children. But the Nuclear Family, if you will, *is merely an idea or model* used as a standard rule of what a family is. The term Nuclear Family was coined by the anthropologist, Robert Murdock in 1949.

The Traditional Nuclear Family is considered middle class in which a woman's primary roles are wife and mother, and a man's primary roles are husband and bread winner.

Because people believe the Traditional Nuclear Family is the "True Family," they compared all other types of families against this model. *The Traditional Nuclear Family does not describe the reality of many families.* In fact, the Nuclear Family is only one of many natural family types in most major societies today.

Yet none of these family types in and of themselves were modeled after what Jesus referred to as the "True Family" which will be discussed further on.

Various *Natural* Family Types

- **Nuclear or Biological Family** – Father, Mother with biological children

- **Traditional Nuclear Family** – A middle class biological family

- **Blended Family** – Remarried couple with biological children from one or both parents. An unmarried parent with children that marries for the first time

- **Single-Parent Family** – Single-Parent with biological or adopted children

- **Child-Free Family** – Married couple without children

- **Family by Adoption** – Married couple with adopted children

- **Foster-Parent Family** – Children living in a Foster Care Home

- **Immediate Family** – Father, Mother, their children, their children's spouses and their grandchildren

- **Extended Family** – From the Immediate Family the Extended Family is from both the father and the mother and includes other relatives related by blood or marriage:

parents, siblings, grandparents, great grandparents, uncles, aunts, cousins, and in-laws.

The most widespread family types in our society today are the intact two-parent family homes, the Biological and Blended families. Followed by the Single-Parent Families with biological or adopted children as well as the two-parent adopted home.

However, there are now more Blended/step Families than any other family group. The current fifty percent rate of divorces occurring whether people are Christians or non-Christians has much to do with the Blended Family growth.

A Blended Family not only takes place when a marriage dissolves and there is a remarriage but it could also take place when an unmarried woman gives birth and later marries a man that is *not* the biological father. Or an unmarried man with child(ren) marries a woman other than the children's mother.

Because of these circumstances less than half of all families are the Traditional Nuclear Family. The Blended Family is no longer the exception but the norm. (See *God's Way and the Blended Family* for additional information.)

When God formed the first family He started with two parents because it was designed to function in a certain manner. Since the seventies, *Single-Parent Families* have been increasing at four to five times the rate of two-parent families. In addition, many families are headed by single mothers, single fathers, grandparents or some other family member are also blessed of God to prosper because God works mightily in these families as well. While I was separated I functioned as a Single-Parent and I watched God become my husband (Isaiah 54:5) and provide, protect and love me as He led my children and me by His Holy Spirit and met all of our needs.

Some single people feel as if they do not have any family because in many cases they have lost family members due to death, divorce or a long-term separation. But they are still a part of a family if they are someone's adult child, someone's mother or father or sibling, and most of all if they are a Child of God then they are a part of the Family of God. In many cases God will give single people a *Spiritual Family because it is not all about the physical blood ties but also about the spiritual ties which in some cases will be a stronger connection.*

Even though this information was shared in the previous chapter the importance of this point needs to be re-emphasized. A body of people living together such as roommates, friends, fraternities, sororities, college dormitories, sport teams, convents, military personnel, firemen, gangs and similar groups may refer to themselves *as a* "family" and may even have some of the same functions, traditions, develop soul ties and become best of friends really caring and loving one another but *nevertheless they are not what God has sanctioned as a "family." A family does not exist merely to fill a void of loneliness, share expenses, experiences, work or even house rules.*

Who God sanctions or approves of as a family in addition to who He refers to as the "True Family" is designed to train up and produce people with godly character that will function for the Kingdom of God within their given society. A family is to bring into place a unit of individuals with like thinking and shared godly morals. In addition, each family member is anointed by God to cause positive change that will affect generations to come. This is why the Lord places emphasis on training up a child in the way they should go, Prov. 22:6.

Family Types that Exist in the Kingdom of God Today

- **God's Family:** Consists of *God's covenant Jewish people,* Gen.12:3; Gen.15:5-14; Exo. 6:7. It also consists of non-Jewish people who are *members of the Body of Christ in the Kingdom of God,* John 3:3; Ephesians 2:14-16. The Kingdom of God includes all those grafted in or adopted from both groups, Jew and non-Jew, into God's family through Christ/Messiah, Eph.1:5; Romans 11:17-19; Gal. 3:24. God's Family also refers to those in *a synagogue and* those in **the Church.** *The Family of God refers to all those who have a* *covenant with the True and Living God, are blessed and operate in the power of God,* Genesis 17:7; Romans 8:17; Gal. 3:16; Psalms 128:1-6; Luke 10:19; I Cor. 6.

- **A Spiritual Family:** Born-again, *Saved people who are divinely connected to a family by God.* They may or may not be biologically related; they may or may not be related by marriage; they may or may not dwell in the same home. The Word says, "…whoever does the will of My Father in heaven…" is a part of His family, Matthew 12:46-50; Mark 3:31-35. A God-fearing family has reverence for His name and walks with the power of God, Psalm 128:1-6; Luke 10:19.

- **The God-Blended Family:** A Blended Family is an intact two parent household (one or both parents bring their children from a previous marriage or relationship) that has been *formed by the Inspiration of Holy Spirit and blended together in marriage.* In addition, they are a family of born-again Christian Believers who are anointed and walk with the power of God, Psalm 128:1-6; Luke 10:19.

- **The One New Man:** A Family from a Divine Perspective. This family is larger than what we would perceive or consider as within the limits of a usual or customary family. On a much broader scale, through Salvation, *The One New Man encompasses people from all over the world that are blended together* as one big joyous family in God's sight, under His protection and authority. *He is our Parent as we belong to His household by His choice and our decision.* **This Family crosses all barriers as people are united regardless of race, creed, ethnic group, color, culture, status or former religion.** This family comprises of and aligns Jew and Gentile and reconciles them back to Father God through the Cross, creating in Himself, *One New Man.* Grafted in by adoption by the blood of Yeshua/Jesus, having become one in Him, making one new quality of humanity out of the two and bringing about covenant restoration, Eph. 2:14-22; Ro.11:11-24; Eph.1:5 and Gal.3:26-29. This *Spiritual Family* is also referred to as *the Body of Christ, the Bride of Christ or the Kingdom of God.*

All people were created by God so He is their Creator but to those who are Saved (have received Salvation) He becomes their "Father" as they are grafted into His Family, Ro.10:9-10; I John 2:2, 12; Eph. 1:5; Romans 11:11-24. In the book of Hebrews 2:11 NIV it says, *"Both the one who makes people holy and those who are made holy are of the same family. So Jesus is not ashamed to call them brothers and sisters."*

"He died for everyone so that those who receive his new life will no longer live to please themselves. Instead, they will live to please Christ, who died and was raised for them," 2 Cor. 5:15 NLT.

We exist because God is a Divine Person and He desired to be in a family relationship with all of us! He told Abraham from the beginning how many descendants he would have which would include God's Family through Christ Jesus, Psalm 89:3-4. In Genesis 15:5 it says, "And He brought him outside [his tent into the starlight] and said, Look now toward the heavens and count the stars – if you are able to number them. Then He said to him, So shall your descendants be."

In Genesis 22:17-18 God told Abraham the following about his Seed and his Descendants,

> In blessing I will bless you and in multiplying I will multiply your descendants like the stars of the heavens and like the sand on the seashore. And your Seed (Heir) will possess the gate of

His enemies. And in your Seed [Christ] shall all the nations of the earth be blessed and [by Him] bless themselves, because you have heard and obeyed My voice.

The "True Family" as Described by Our Lord

There is still another type of family that is greater than all of these listed. The Word of God refers to it as *the True Family*. Furthermore, the True Family can be applied and incorporated into each and every one of the natural family types.

It is a type of family that is overlooked by most societies when defining what a family is. Because the True Family does not fit into the scope of a traditional Greek mindset or custom. Therefore, limitations are set and many people are dismissed, forgotten, left out and persecuted in their natural family circle because of ignorance of who God refers to as the "True Family."

The following is a great illustration of The Father's Family or God's Family as demonstrated by Jesus when He defines who is in *His Spiritual Family* which He also referred to as *His True family.*

An example of a True Family is Found in Matthew 12:46-50,

> Jesus was still speaking to the people when behold, His mother and brothers stood outside, seeking to speak to Him. *Someone said to Him, Listen! Your mother and Your brothers are standing outside, seeking to speak to You.* But He replied to the man who told Him, Who is My mother, and who are My brothers? And stretching out His hand toward [not only the twelve disciples but all] His adherents, He said, Here are My mother and My brothers. **For whoever does the Will of My Father in heaven is My brother and sister and mother!** (Emphasis added.)

Hebrew 2:10-11 NIV further says,

> In bringing many sons and daughters to glory, it was fitting that God, for whom and through whom everything exists, should make the pioneer of their salvation perfect through what he suffered. *Both the one who makes people holy and those who are made holy are of the same family.* So Jesus is not ashamed to call them brothers and sisters. (Emphasis added.)

The "True Family" is the Family of God, a Biblical and Spiritual Family. It is at the forefront of marriage, family values, traditions and customs.

The Spiritual Family will be used in the Last Days against the kingdom of darkness with the anointing that is on their lives. In addition, the prayers of the husband and wife are the most powerful prayers on earth. They are one in the Spirit and when in agreement and aligned with God they and their family will overpower the divisive tactics of the wicked one. (See *Chapter Eight* in this resource as well as *God's Way and Spiritual Warfare* for more revelation of how an anointed family of God will be mightily used in the Last Days by Almighty God.)

The term "Family of God" can be used to describe the natural Jewish relationship with God. It is also used in reference to the Body of Christ which is a part of the Family of God by adoption, Ephesians 1:5. The Body of Christ includes anyone who has received Jesus as Messiah (Yeshua HaMashiach in Hebrew) as their Lord and Savior. And finally, the Body of Christ *is* the Kingdom of God.

Although on a smaller and more personal note it also describes a family located within an individual home. The Family of God is not based *on traditions and morals alone* but on the fact at the *Head* of this type of family there is a *High Priest.*

One that is the same yesterday, today and forevermore and Who understands family, Hebrews 13:8. His name is Jesus and He has the power to perfect these unions as willing hearts are yielded to His precepts and instructions.

In our hearts when we are willing to live by faith we can be successful in our families. Remember, it is not only what you *believe* that matters, it is how you *behave* in accordance with what you believe that will make the difference.

God did not design marriage with a basic contract in mind. He drew up a contract between a man and a woman, but nevertheless, He sees a covenant. Wherein two separate wills are willing to die to themselves, which basically means, to not focus on your own efforts but rather lean on God and come in agreement with Him as He is a part of this covenant and operate with the faith of Christ (The Anointed One).

Galatians 2:20 tells us,

> I have been crucified with Christ [in Him I have shared His crucifixion]; it is no longer I who live, but Christ (the Messiah) lives in me; *and the life I now live in the body I live by faith* in (by adherence to and reliance on and complete trust in) the Son of God, Who loved me and gave Himself up for me. (Emphasis added.)

Then they are to look to Jesus as their Head and trust the Holy Spirit will be there to teach them and bring them into all truth about everything concerns their lives and the lives of their love ones.

When operating with biblical principles your priorities change, your interests change, values change and habits change for the good. Love, trust and fairness are handled differently and there is less taking each other for granted, less isolation, rejection and ignoring of children. *As a matter of fact, one of the greatest things a father can do for his children is to love their mother (his wife).*

With God in the picture people in the family can have their own personal relationship with reverence and respect for Him. If they are humble enough (admitting to themselves they need a Savior) to receive instructions from His Holy Spirit, then the Holy Spirit will enable (grace) them to do what Father God has purposed for them to do. This will make all the difference in the world for their household. Where there is relationship, people are more prone to want to please God rather than spend a lot of time trying to be a people pleaser.

God is first in a true Family of God. He will cause everything to line up and move into position at the appointed time so whatever is needed for your life it can be released. In this type of family your focus changes and everything is seen more clearly which can produce a peace. As a result, there is less stress, less worry because you will become more trusting (leaning on, relying on and having confidence) as you rest in the Lord, Prov. 3:5-7.

The following will illustrate how Jesus was rejected in His home town because He was only associated with His natural family and not with the Family of God – His Spiritual Family. Jesus visited His home town where He grew up and the people there knew He was a part of this *natural* family. They knew His mother Mary, His brothers and sisters and that He grew up as a carpenter's son. And because of this *they reasoned in their own minds* (reasoning brings you into the devil's territory) and they rejected Jesus' spiritual authority. They could not understand how He had so much wisdom. They found it hard to believe He could perform miracles, Matthew 13:53-58.

When He was rejected in His own home town, Jesus said to them, "A prophet is not without honor except in his own country and in his own house" Matthew 13:57.

"God said let Us [Father, Son and Holy Spirit] make mankind in Our image, after Our likeness, and **let them have complete authority**… and over all of the earth… He created him, male and female He created them," Genesis 1:26-27 and 2:7; 22; Hebrews 1:2-3 and 11:3.

In the book of John, it says *God is a Spirit* (**a Spiritual Being**) and we who were made in His image are spiritual beings as well. We possess a soul (mind, will and emotions) and our spirit lives in a body. We are part spirit, soul and body as stated in the book of I Thessalonians 5:23. Furthermore, we are of a Spiritual Family based primarily on what God has said.

John 4:23-24 tells us,

> A time will come, however, indeed it is already here, when the true (genuine) worshipers will worship the Father in spirit and in truth (reality); for the Father is seeking just such people as these as His worshipers. **God is a Spirit (Spiritual Being)** and those who worship Him must worship Him in spirit and in truth (reality). (Emphasis added).

As a Spiritual Being the Holy Spirit communicates with our spirit once we receive our Salvation and are Born-again and it will increase in different ways once we have the *Infilling of the Holy Spirit* (after we are baptized with the Holy Spirit), Acts 1:5, 8.

Briefly what it means to have the Infilling of the Holy Spirit which is also known as the Baptism in the Holy Spirit (Acts 2:1-4) as listed above, is one of the key qualities a Family of God acquires. We know the "church" is the person who is in Christ not the building, although the building is also referred to as the church. After Salvation the Infilling of the Holy Spirit is the second most important impartation from God to all Believers.

"The church received the Spirit at a moment God chose. The church had not become more committed, prayerful, or spiritual in and of itself. *The gift of the Spirit was entirely a matter of grace*. In the Upper Room the Spirit was given each person, as the tongues of fire separating and resting on each person demonstrated. The Spirit represented a new commitment of God to the covenant relationship summarized in Lev. 26:12. Three miraculous signs accompanied the giving of the Spirit: the sound of a wind (Greek pneuma means both wind and Spirit); tongues of fire (tongues point to the worldwide mission of the church to preach the gospel); and speaking 'in other tongues,' which also pointed to the preaching mission." [1] Acts 2:1-4 paraphrased.

Speaking in an unknown tongue is a supernatural spiritual language is for all who are Born-again Believers. It is a language of men and angels which reveals the mysteries of God no one understands except God, also it offers great benefits to whosoever receives and uses it, I Cor.13:1; 14:2.

Furthermore, as we live and walk by the Spirit looking to the Holy Spirit to help us become more and more like Jesus, it is during this process we experience a renewing of our minds, Romans12:2. As we begin to die to the flesh (the old way of thinking) we start to take on the will of Christ and walk in the Spirit of God as stated in the following passage.

Galatians 5:16-26 says,

> But I say, walk *and* live [habitually] in the [Holy] Spirit [responsive to *and* controlled *and* guided by the Spirit]; then you will certainly not gratify the cravings *and* desires of the flesh (of human nature without God) ...

This is how other people will know we are a part of the Family of God because we will have the glory of God on us as we demonstrate the fruit of the Spirit, Galatians 5:22-23 and the power of God in Acts 2.

God's family is spiritual and they are alive in Him. "People who are not saved are spiritually dead. This means they are not able to enjoy communion with God or perceive and follow the intuitive promptings of the Holy Spirit. These people are limited to their natural or intellectual knowledge and to their common sense; they cannot enjoy the privilege and power of living by revelation.

But, *when we have been Born-again and are alive spiritually, God can speak to us and show us things we could not have known without divine revelation* ...If you will be diligent to seek Him and listen to His voice, He will lead you supernaturally. He will teach you how to fulfill His purposes for your life – and they may be far greater than anything you are currently trained to do or could ever imagine.[2]

The One New Man is A Part of the Family of God

If you consider yourself to be a part of the **Family of God** because of the Finished Work the Messiah did at the Cross it would mean you have declared you are a part of the **One New Man,** Eph. 2:14-18. God desires Jews and Gentiles come together in Messiah and worship as One New Man in faith.

Furthermore, as a One New Man in the Kingdom of God you could be referred to as a Christian, a Believer, a Messianic Jew, Born-again, a Saint, a Child of God, Saved, a son or daughter of God, sister or brother in the Lord and an Evangelical to name a few terms used in the Kingdom of God. But before Christendom began all of *the first Believers were Jewish followers in the Messiah,* the Anointed One of Israel and His Church at that time was called "The Way."

These two groups which worshipped together and operated in the fivefold ministry gifts during the early church in the first century witnessed many miracles, power and blessings as a result of coming together in Yeshua/Jesus. The two groups were separated during the Dark Ages. This was never God's will or desire.

We are called and destined to be one in the Kingdom of God, worshipping the One True Living God. There are benefits for both the Jewish Believer and the Non-Jewish Believer because as we continue moving forward insight, fresh revelation and understanding of the Old Covenant of ***what was*** *concealed,* to the understanding and revelation of *what is being revealed* in the New Covenant will change. It will advance God's Kingdom and give us life to the full as He purposed from the beginning, John 10:10.

The Old and New Covenants are respectfully known as the Holy Bible. The Old Testament in Hebrew is known as the Tanakh. The first five books are referred to as the Torah. The New Testament in Hebrew is called B'rit Hadashah.

Ephesians 2:12-20 explains the One New Man, Jew and Gentile in Messiah,

[Remember] that you were at that time separated (living apart) from Christ [excluded from all part in Him], utterly estranged and outlawed from the rights of Israel as a nation, and strangers with no share in the sacred compacts of the [Messianic] promise [with no knowledge of or right in God's agreements, His covenants]. *And you had no hope (no promise); you were in the world without God. But now in Christ Jesus, you who once were [so] far away, through (by, in) the blood of Christ have been brought near.* For He is [Himself] our peace (our bond of unity and harmony). *He has made us both [Jew and Gentile] one [body], and has broken down (destroyed, abolished) the hostile dividing wall between us,* by abolishing in His [own crucified] flesh the enmity [caused by] the Law with its decrees and ordinances [which He annulled]; that He from the two might create in Himself **ONE NEW MAN** [one new quality of humanity out of the two], so making peace. And *[He designed] to reconcile to God both [Jew and Gentile, united] in a single body by means of His cross, thereby killing the mutual enmity and bringing the feud to an end.* And He came and preached the glad tidings of peace to you who were afar off and [peace] to those who were near. For it is through Him that we both [whether far off or near] now have an introduction (access) by one [Holy] Spirit to the Father [so that we are able to approach Him]. Therefore you are no longer outsiders (exiles, migrants, and aliens, excluded from the rights of citizens), but you now share citizenship with the saints (God's own people, consecrated and set apart for Himself); and you belong to God's [own] household. You are built upon the foundation of the apostles and prophets with Christ Jesus Himself the chief Cornerstone. (Emphasis added.)

"Christt destroyed the division between Jews and non-Jews, providing all people the opportunity to be saved by grace. In His death He reconciled sinners to God, destroying our hatred for Him. Thus Jesus/Yeshua opened the way for us to live in God's presence. The Holy Spirit is the presence of God with us. Jesus founded the church and is the uniting power for it" [3] Ephesians 2:14-22.

While the Jews seek power and the Greeks seek after wisdom the following scriptures demonstrate what both the Jew and Greek sought after were found in the Messiah (Christ), the Anointed One, Jesus/Yeshua HaMashiach. He was sent by Father God and He reconciled both the Jew and the Gentile (Greek, the nations) back to God. He empowered all who received Him with authority and wisdom to do all things through Christ Who would strengthen them to accomplish their assignments or purpose on earth, Phil. 4:13.

What You Seek is Found in Christ the Messiah, I Corinthians 1:22, 24-25 tells us,

> For while Jews [demandingly] ask for signs *and* miracles and Greeks pursue philosophy *and* wisdom, …But to those who are called, whether Jew or Greek (Gentile), Christ [is] the Power of God and the Wisdom of God. [This is] because the foolish thing [that has its source in] God is wiser than men, and the

weak thing [that springs] from God is stronger than men.

Furthermore, it says in I Cor. 1:18 "For the story *and* message of the cross is sheer absurdity *and* folly to those who are perishing *and* on their way to perdition, but to us who being saved it is the [manifestation of] the power of God." This is further confirmed in verse 21, "For when the world with all its earthly wisdom failed to perceive *and* recognize *and* know God by means of its own philosophy, God in His wisdom was pleased through the foolishness of preaching [salvation, procured by Christ and to be had through Him], to save those who believed (who clung to and trusted in and relied on Him)." Also read I Corinthians 1:27-31 for additional insight on this point.

As a marriage between one man, one woman and God (YHVH) is valid in God's sight, so is the union of Jew and Gentile. They are one in God through His Son Jesus and the union is valid so the Father can embrace the individuals as the One New Man in Messiah, Eph. 2:14.

Earthly marriage is a type and shadow of the spiritual marriage and union God has formed with His people the Jews. Now all those (whether Jew or Gentile) who received His sacrifice through offering His Son have become fellow citizens and have acquired a covenant with Almighty God.

There are Three Different People Groups on the Earth

The Jews
The Gentile (The Nations; the Greeks)
The Church (Body of Christ; One New Man)

The Word of God in I Cor. 10:32 NKJV says, "Give no offense, either to the Jews or to the Greeks or to the church of God." Recognizing the three different people groups on the earth.

The Jewish people were chosen by God and given the Abrahamic Covenant, Genesis 12:2-3. In this Covenant the people are entitled to wisdom, ideas, strategies, favor, provision, businesses, protection, good health and wholeness. In this covenant God will empower you to have wealth that He may establish His covenant which He swore to your fathers, Deuteronomy 8:18. Furthermore, if they kept the Ten Commandments (chose to live upright according to the Law which were instructions on how to live) they could have a good life on earth.

This proved to be impossible and they learned it was faith that would be the determining factor of how they lived before God which would be pleasing to Him. It is written in Galatians 3:7, "Know and understand that it is [really] the people [who live] by faith who are [the true] sons of Abraham." Those that were righteous in faith, when they passed, they would go into a holding place (some call a place of

Truth or Abraham's Bosom) and *kept from the eternal fire of hell* (Matt. 25:41; Matt. 10:28; Rev.20:12-15) located in the bowels of the earth *until* the Redeemer/Jesus was resurrected from the grave.

After the Resurrection those that were in Abraham's Bosom were taken to heaven. Afterwards hell enlarged itself. Now all must receive the Savior Yeshua/Jesus to enter into the Kingdom of Heaven, Acts 2:21; Romans 10:9-10; I John 2:2, 12.

The Gentile is a person who is not of Jewish decent. Other terms to express a Gentile would be secular, worldly, the nations, carnal, Greek, Egypt and so on. Greek and Egypt are not referring to the people in those countries. Those are terms used in the Bible linked with those who captured Israel and it meant they were not Jews but at one time were enemies. *Gentiles do not have a covenant with the Living God of Abraham, Isaac and Jacob.* When they pass, their soul is condemned and they go directly into hell basically because of unbelief in the One who was sent to save them from their sins, John 8:44, John 10:10, Matthew 25:41.

The Church, Christian Believers (Jew or Gentile) are those who have received Jesus the Christ - Yeshua HaMashiach (in Hebrew), as their Lord and Savior. Instantly they become "a new creation (a new creature altogether); the old [previous moral and spiritual condition] has passed away. Behold, the fresh *and* new has come!" 2 Cor. 5:17. At that moment they, the Gentile Believers, are grafted into the Family of God as they become heirs of Abraham's Seed. They receive the Abrahamic covenant as the Jews have which includes protection and the blessings of Abraham as they live by faith, Gal. 3:8-9.

In addition, both Jew and Gentile in Messiah have become the One New Man, Eph. 2:14-20. Under the New Covenant all receive eternal life, John 3:16; Titus 3:6-7. When the Messiah came He fulfilled the Law and gave the New Covenant, Matthew 5:17; Matthew 26:26-29; Luke 22:20. Also, the body of Christ is in the Kingdom of God which Jesus preached was at hand.

In the Old Testament (The Tanakh in Hebrew), in Jeremiah 31:31-33 the LORD said He was going to make a New Covenant with the House of Israel. This was revealed in the New Testament (in Hebrew B'rit Hadashah), Romans 2:28-29; Romans 3:28; Mt. 26:28; Gal. 2:16-21; Gal. 3:7-14.

Therefore, *through Salvation people were grafted into the Family of God by adoption Eph. 1:5.* The Spirit of Adoption is the Holy Spirit and the Spirit testifies with our spirit we are God's children, Romans 8:15-16.

The word adoption in a spiritual sense basically means a person is brought into the Family of God, even though they were previously without any covenant with God. Like all of us who are born-again (saved) we were sinners and separated from Father God after the fall of mankind. But God in His mercy and grace redeemed us, purchased us and brought us into His presence once again through the blood of His only beloved Son, Jesus.

Do Jewish People Need Salvation which gives Access to YHVH and His New Covenant even though they have a Covenant with the God of Abraham, Isaac and Jacob?

The Holy Scriptures Explains the Answer through Romans 3:21-31 NIV (Emphasis added.)

> But now apart from the law the righteousness of God has been made known, to which the Law and the Prophets testify. This righteousness is given through faith in Jesus Christ to all who believe. *There is no difference between Jew and Gentile, for all have sinned and fall short of the glory of God,* and all are justified freely by his grace through the redemption that came by Christ Jesus. *God presented Christ as a sacrifice of atonement, through the shedding of His blood –to be received by faith.* He did this to demonstrate his righteousness, because in his forbearance he had left the sins committed beforehand unpunished –He did it to demonstrate his righteousness at the present time, so as to be just and the one who justifies those who have faith in

Jesus. *Where, then, is boasting? It is excluded.* Because of what law? The law that requires work? No, *because of the law that requires faith.* For we maintain that a person is justified by faith apart from the works of the law. Or is God the God of Jews only? Is he not the God of Gentiles too? Yes, of Gentiles too, since there is only one God, who will justify the circumcised by faith and the uncircumcised through that same faith. Do we, then, nullify the law by this faith? Not at all! *Rather, we uphold the law.*

We are justified both Jew and Gentile only when our faith is in Jesus (Yeshua). This excludes therefore all pride and boasting about keeping the Law (instructions for good deeds) that requires works because *the only law that is required is the law that requires faith!* A person is justified by faith apart from the works of the law freely because of what Jesus/Yeshua did for us. Also see Romans 9:30-32 and Galatians 2:15-16.

Children of God Includes Both Jew and Gentile According to Galatians 3:26-29,

For in Christ Jesus you are all sons of God through faith. For as many [of you] as were baptized into Christ [into a spiritual union and communion with Christ, the Anointed One, the Messiah] have put on (clothed yourselves with) Christ. There is [now no distinction] neither Jew nor Greek, there is neither slave nor free, there is not male and female; for you are all one in Christ Jesus. And if you belong to Christ [are in Him Who is Abraham's Seed], then you are Abraham's offspring and [spiritual] heirs according to promise.

Furthermore, we are called to uphold the Law because Jesus came and not only *fulfilled the Law* but ***the law was written on our hearts by Almighty God.*** That Law in the New Covenant is found in Matthew 22:27-40. It is called the first and greatest commandment. It says, "You shall love the Lord your God with all your heart and with all your soul and with all your mind (intellect). This is the great and first commandment. And a second is like it: You shall love your neighbor as [you do] yourself. These two commandments sum up *and* upon them depend all the Law and the Prophets."

Jesus announced the New Covenant at Passover before He became the Passover Lamb. He Who died and was resurrected which set the New Covenant into effect Romans 11:11-24; John 1:17; Jeremiah 31:33, Galatians 3:7-14; I Cor. 5:7; Matthew 26:28.

As stated above, the Lord gave a New Covenant for Israel in Jeremiah 31:31-33. **The New Covenant includes Eternal Life through Salvation.** Upon passing, the Believer will be escorted directly into Heaven by angels Luke 16:22. In the New Covenant people are filled with the Spirit of God and given authority over sickness, circumstances in life and a sustaining joy because they believe and live by faith. (See *Chapter Ten* for more details regarding the Benefits of being in the Family of God.)

Upon a person passing, in the Tanakh or Old Covenant only a holding place was provided until Messiah came. *Since He did come, died and rose from the grave the righteous that were in a holding place called Abraham's Bosom, Luke 16.22, were transported to heaven.* Hell enlarged itself when they were removed from across the gulf where the righteous were held until redemption Luke 16:22-26. Therefore, those righteous in Christ (saved) do not go to a holding place in hell any longer. That place no longer exist since the Resurrection of the Messiah.

Jesus was given all authority in heaven and earth Matthew 28:18. *He took back the keys to death, hell and the grave and gave the authority to all Believers whether Jew or Gentile,* Luke 10:19. They now have a way of escape from the pit of hell John 8:44; John 10:10 and Matthew 25:41. Only those who are foolish enough to not believe the price that was paid by the Messiah/Mashiach will be doomed to outer darkness for eternity, I Corinthians 2:14; John 6:63-64.

Jesus Himself summed it all up in John 14:6 when He said, ***"I am the Way, and the Truth and the Life; no one comes to the Father except by*** *(through) Me" emphasis added.* Also see John 14:9-10. In addition, I John 2:23 NIV says, *"No one who denies the Son has the Father; whoever acknowledges the Son has the Father also."*

Therefore, "Be still, and know that I am God; I will be exalted among the nations, I will be exalted in the earth," Psalm 46:10. Let us set aside the *opinions* of men in whatever form it comes to us. Whether it is through a minister or through the Talmud, nothing supersedes the written Word of God with the breath of the Spirit of God upon it giving those words life. And nothing supersedes His Glory! For all the glory belongs to Him!

The Family Home is a Part of Its Nation

The home is a basic unit and cannot be separated from the health of its nation. Families determine the condition of its nation, therefore, if the home goes the nation will follow. The church or body of Jesus Christ, on a broader scale is known as the Kingdom of God. It is the only institution that is actually lifting-up in prayer, America and all countries around the world where there are Believers in Jesus/Yeshua. This prayer is for a great "Awakening" (people returning to God and making Him and His ways first in their lives).

As a result of these prayers from *church families* which are made up of *individual families*, these prayers will cause God to move greatly on your country's behalf and in the lives of those who believe. So even though a society has declined, the

Believer within a given society can still experience peace, joy, abundance, good health and overall be blessed in the midst of any storm life brings.

Because *the Kingdom of God expands beyond your physical location. Christians around the world are a part of the Kingdom of God* and whatever country or individual that is praying *God is no respecter of persons.* He will answer with an "Awakening" for that nation as well as for those individuals.

The Kingdom of God, which is also a government, is primarily made-up from family units within the Body of Christ. Like any government their role is to protect one's rights to pursue legitimate goods (in this case spiritual and natural). The Kingdom of God will do its part for its citizens (the Believers) because it shows the most promise to do so having the Spirit of God at the forefront. How is that? The Kingdom of God is located within each Born-again Believer (Christian) and its attributes are righteousness, peace and joy in the Holy Spirit Romans 14:17. Therefore, it will always strive to do what is right and what is right is measured by the Word of God. When the will of God is in effect it will change the individual, the family and the society the family dwells in.

The family is the backbone for all societies. God through His Kingdom of people *"the Church or the Ecclesia"* not through a building or denomination, but individuals who follow Christ and pray. They will strengthen our nation again, help purify and restore it **by giving way to a new**

and more productive society. Because education is an essential component of any society a more godly and productive educational system will be produced as well. *As a result, godly education will produce godly citizens which will produce godly political representatives and in turn produce a godly government.* Also, as godly judges *regain* positions in the higher courts, these actions altogether will affect the well-being of a Family of God.

Since our Lord and Savior is ***about Relationship and not*** about ***religion,*** any family that chooses the biblical guidelines, chooses *God's way.* They will have qualities that can produce successful results and cause their families to continue to prosper (be whole in every area) and to have a wonderful home in a time when most families will be totally dysfunctional and falling completely apart.

The Family of God is how God intended a family to function with definite roles, goals, teaching the next generation about God and the family being led by the Spirit of God. If the leaders (parents) know how to relate (communicate) to one another and to their children it will strengthen the family. Having the understanding and knowledge of how to relate in a relationship as a married couple, as parents, as a parent to a child and a child to a parent, siblings to one another and to the extended family members in a loving and positive way will be the result of following biblical principles.

A Family of God should exercise many different qualities that are based on the Word of

God which will literally strengthen them as individuals, as a married couple and as a family. (See *Chapter One* for more information in this area.)

Key Tips for Strength and Recovery

Mark 12:30 Emphasizes to Place God First,

> And you shall love the Lord your God out of *and* with your whole heart and out of *and* with all your soul (your life) and out of *and* with all your mind (with your faculty of thought and your moral understanding) and out of *and* with all your strength. *This is the first and principal commandment.* (Emphasis added.)

As you love God with all your strength you will be strengthened. To love God with all your strength is to use your influence, possessions, resources and wealth as well as your position in life you were blessed with to share, bless and help someone else. In doing so you are honoring and showing love towards God. Your hands are His hands on this earth. (One interpretation of hands is they represent the work of ministry which is not limited to the four walls of a church building but is for every Believer to operate in, in the midst of their purpose).

Consider Expressing Love God's Way as seen in the Love Chapter, I Corinthians 13:4-8,

Love endures long *and* is patient and kind; **love never is** envious *nor* boils over with jealousy, is not boastful *or* vainglorious, does not display itself haughtily. It is not conceited (arrogant and inflated with pride); it is not rude (unmannerly) *and* does not act unbecomingly. Love **(God's love in us)** does not insist on its own rights *or* its own way, *for* it is not self-seeking; it is not touchy *or* fretful *or* resentful; it takes no account of the evil done to it [it pays no attention to a suffered wrong]. It does not rejoice at injustice and unrighteousness, but **rejoices when right *and* truth prevail**. Love bears up under anything *and* everything that comes, is ever **ready to believe the best of every person**, its hopes are fadeless under all circumstances, and it endures everything [without weakening]. **Love never fails** [never fades out or becomes obsolete or comes to an end] ... (Emphasis added.)

Believers Keep Your Heart Pure Before God So Communication Will Stay Open

Everyone makes mistakes and fall short of the glory of God, Romans 3:23. And the process that will bring you back into right standing with God is Repentance. Because of repentance we do not have to live with condemnation, guilt, shame, anger or torment. The Blood of the Lamb (Jesus is the Lamb of God, I Corinthians 5:7) washes away our sin and we are free to be at peace and to have joy.

Repentance simply means you have changed your mind and you have made a decision to go in another direction, the direction of righteousness, I John 1:9. The word repent means to turn around and go back; "Pent" means the highest. When we repent to God we are returning to the highest place of relationship mankind has with Him. Go back to that place in the glory that you occupy, Ephesians 2:6.

Therefore, when you are ready to repent you go before God with a sorrowful heart for the sin that was committed and ask for forgiveness and then repent, 2 Corinthians 7:10 and 2 Peter 3:9.

Now by faith receive your forgiveness and continue with God. And when you slip, fall, make a mistake that is sinful you do the same process. And after repenting if guilt or shame or any negative emotion tries to come and torment you, know it is not from God and command it to leave in Jesus' name.

In addition, you can ask the Lord to strengthen you in the area where you are weak. Read the living words in the Bible, they will strengthen you. Spend time developing your personal relationship with Him.

He is a loving God and will extend His grace and mercy as many times as needed.

(See *God's Way and Knowing the King* for further information on developing and maintaining a personal relationship with our Savior.)

Chapter 3
Delegated Authority is Part of God's Order

With God's delegated authority in our lives, our lives flow better. We have better role models, a decent society in which to live and a certain amount of freedom to express our beliefs and practice our rights. As we listen and follow through to give honor and respect to our delegated authorities *we set an example by having the right attitude and submission toward authority before our children. They will learn we all must obey rules, regulations, and guidelines.*

As we respect and pay attention to signs and information posted by these authorities we are recognizing *God placed these authorities before us for our safety and to promote our joy.* In addition, because we honor the signs and whatnot we will not hinder our ability to hear God's voice and receive His instructions. ***We honor God when we honor the authority around us. In this we are exercising true freedom and true liberty in Christ.***

The following is a list of some of the delegated authority figures that will influence most of our lives: our parents or guardians, spiritual leaders, teachers on all levels, employers, public servants, the laws of the land, respect for the office of the President, the government, as well as state and local officials, civil authorities, all level of judges in the judicial system, the armed forces, our police officers, traffic control, FBI agents and so forth.

Romans 13:1-6 is the Biblical Recording of our Civil Delegated Authorities,

Let every person be loyally subject to the governing (civil) authorities. For there is no authority except from God [by His permission, His sanction], and those that exist do so by God's appointment. Therefore he who resists and sets himself up against the authorities resists what God has appointed and arranged [in divine order]. And those who resist will bring down judgment upon themselves [receiving the penalty due them]. For civil authorities are not a terror to [people of] good conduct, but to [those of] bad behavior. Would you have no dread of him who is in authority? Then do what is right and you will receive his approval and commendation. For he is God's servant for your good. But if you do wrong, [you should dread him and] be afraid, for he does not bear and wear the sword for nothing. He is God's servant to execute His wrath (punishment, vengeance) on the wrongdoer. Therefore one must be subject, not only to avoid God's wrath and escape punishment, but also as a matter of principle and for the sake of conscience. For this same reason you pay taxes, for [the civil authorities] are official servants under God, devoting themselves to attending to this very service. (Emphasis added.)

I Timothy 2:1-3 tells us we are to Pray for Our Civil Leaders,

First of all, then, I admonish and urge that *petitions, prayers, intercessions, and thanksgivings be offered on behalf of all men.* For kings and all who are in positions of authority or high responsibility, that [outwardly] we may pass a quiet and undisturbed life [and inwardly] a peaceable one in all godliness and reverence and seriousness in every way. For such [praying] is good *and* right, and [it is] pleasing *and* acceptable to God our Savior. (Emphasis added.)

Hebrews 13:17 is a Biblical Recording for Our Spiritual Authority,

Obey your spiritual leaders and submit to them [continually recognizing their authority over you], for they are constantly keeping watch over your souls and guarding your spiritual welfare, as men who will have to render an account [to their trust]. [Do your part to] let them do this with gladness and not with sighing and groaning, for that would not be profitable to you [either].

2 Corinthians 1:24 has Additional Comments on Spiritual Authority,

Not that we have dominion [over you] and lord it over your faith, but [rather that we work with you as] fellow laborers [to promote] your joy, for in [your] faith (in your strong and welcome conviction or belief that Jesus is the Messiah, through Whom we obtain eternal salvation in the Kingdom of God) you stand firm.

Some reasons spiritual authority exist, is to increase our strength and joy, to help us remain sensitive to the leading of the Holy Spirit to receive instructions and directions as well as fellowship with God. As we learn to obey (follow the instructions) and submit to the delegated authorities God has placed in our lives we also learn how to be in authority. *In other words, we must know both how to be under authority and be in authority to be effective in the Kingdom of God.*
True leaders first have learned how to submit to authority before they attempt to lead. When we

really have learned to yield to His authority in the land it will become easier to recognize it whether it is in our home, work place, schools, military, courts or any other institution. As we yield out of respect for the office God has set in place God will honor our obedience. **Realize you are not being subject to the person in the office but to the anointing on the office that God has ordained for a person to oversee.**

Hebrews 5:8-9 says, "Although He was a Son, He learned [active, special] obedience through what He suffered..." Some of us never learned to yield to spiritual or civil authority and in not doing so never achieved the destiny purposed for our lives. *God is no respecter of persons what He asks of one He asks of all and that is to respect who He has put into place for His purposes which will work together for the good of all people.* If we are subject to our Heavenly Father then we must also be subject to His delegated authority for they represent Him and are responsible for their assignments from Him, therefore, *in God's eyes if we reject His delegated authority we are rejecting Him.*

Furthermore, God will not entrust His authority to self-righteous prideful people who seek the glory for themselves. Hidden pride always comes out. But He will entrust His authority to those who are set apart and sanctified for His use. People in authority are often alone because they are set apart and cannot do as others do in many things and still be mightily used of God.

We are to appoint, elect and vote people into leadership roles that know Him, believe in His Word, which is His will and plan, so good leaders will rule over the people. Then the people will rejoice otherwise they will groan and sigh. This God-given instruction works together for the good and protection of all. Proverbs 29:2 says, "When the [uncompromisingly] righteous are in authority, the people rejoice; but when the wicked man rules, the people groan and sigh." That is one reason why we are called to pray for our civil leaders I Timothy 2:1-2.

True freedom is to have peace while obeying the authority God has placed in your life. True freedom is not doing whatever whenever you wish to do something, that will only lead to misery and a sense of loss of control for your life and cause your life to eventually lose meaning.

True freedom is liberty in Christ; to set forth to accomplish your vision and fulfill the purpose of your life as it is given by God while obeying the laws of the land and delegated authority in your life.

Most people need guidelines and boundaries in order to be held accountable to someone other than themselves. People also need a meaningful support system of others in their lives. The God we serve is a God of relationship; therefore, He desires we fellowship, love and help one another. The first people on earth had a personal relationship with God and with each other.

We as parents can add to being a positive role model when we decide to pray, vote and obey our leaders, judges, employers, our children's teachers, community business owners and politicians instead of criticizing and judging them especially in front of our children. This will show them a constructive way of living even though there may be unpleasant conditions in our lives because of certain policies and laws. Let them see you are still trusting God to make the necessary changes to improve any given situation or unfair policies or regulations that are beyond your control.

God has the answers to all problems and as we continue to pray and wait with the right attitude and expectations about decisions of those in authority over and around us, God will move in the situation. He will cause the necessary changes to policies and rules and for overall improvements. This is the answer to the prayers of His people.

God is willing to change the hearts of men and to give instructions to show them a better way, and open new doors as He performs miracles. As we watch Him work on our behalf because we decided to obey the laws of the land and respect the authority in our own lives, we become the role models our spouses, children, extended family, neighbors, co-workers, associates, and friends need to see and have in their lives.

Understand some in authority will not always validate or appreciate you. Still, you can receive affirmation and appreciation from somewhere else such as your spouse, family or friends. Right now, be a blessing and learn what God would have you to learn while you are under a certain authority, pass the test and move forward.

On the other hand, a poor example of not respecting delegated authority before your children would be to live unholy. Going about cursing your jobs, employers, supervisors, managers, teachers and civil authorities and coming against the very provisions that were made for you. This would also extend to working in your career or if you own your own business and you are always upset with your employees or the government because of the taxes or whatever is affecting your business.

In any event as we make a conscious decision to honor delegated authority and operate within God's guidelines it will add to our lives, set an example for our families as it teaches them godly principles and integrity while building godly character.

Family Order and Delegated Authority

Parent(s) should be able to come in agreement, especially in areas of guidance and discipline for their children. Consideration should be given as to how they will bring up their children in the Word of God. Parents need to consider how they will prepare their offspring to have the life God purposed for them to have. A great life, living obedient in the will of God so they will not be led astray by false doctrines, the occult, worldly living or any peer pressure.

Communication is a key element in the healing process because *healing comes about when people talk and gain understanding and revelation.* Create a Christ-centered forum for family meetings. A Christ-centered forum will include opening the meeting in prayer, including God in the meeting, sharing praise reports (things God has done for you), discussing the business at hand and closing with prayer.

In these meetings everyone in the family is given an opportunity to discuss their hopes, visions, dreams and give praise reports if they choose to do so. This is also an effective way for family members to generate ideas, hear announcements, changes, updates, family goals, discuss family vacations, outings, events and any changes with the family guidelines (house rules).

In addition, all family members should be able to voice their opinions, share ideas, express or vent their feelings, concerns, complaints, grievances and freely release their frustrations using respectful words as much as possible. Furthermore, they are not blamed, condemned or criticized as they vent and/or say what is on their heart.

Also, allow family members to volunteer to speak and share. Never try to make them voice their feelings if they are not ready or comfortable with the setting or certain people being in the room they are not comfortable with or willing to open up their heart in front of. If they sense the family meeting is "not for real" they more than likely won't say anything or participate in any way. At the next family meeting they may now sense this is something they may want to do if only to have a chance to speak their mind and not be persecuted for it.

It is also important after the meeting not to criticize or make anyone feel uncomfortable but to continue to show the love of God. Let them know it is His love they can draw their strength and needs from. There is personal sacrifice involved when we decide and are committed to show love to others. There is always a cost involved whether it is our time, resources, effort and/or money. However, *the reward we receive from loving others is greater than the cost* because we have chosen to do something unto the Lord and do it God's way.

Hold family meetings as often as your family believes it is necessary, once a week, once every two weeks or once a month. The family meeting should include a plan of action and a follow-up at a family meeting to monitor progress in the areas where reasonable change has been requested by a family member or the entire family.

The parents can set-up the guidelines for their home and discuss them before sharing them at a family meeting. This is important because parents need to be in agreement and on one accord. Being in agreement will maintain a sense of security for their household. They should not voice their disagreements regarding the guidelines in front of their children because they were surprised or caught off-guard about a suggestion the other parent requested.

It is important for the parents to be in agreement with the guidelines (house rules) they feel comfortable with especially if they are a Blended Family. Furthermore, *parents should not compromise their godly beliefs, morals, or show favoritism concerning the family guidelines.*

If someone has a concern in between meetings, of course they should be able to come to the parent at any time. If they had a suggestion that involved others then they would bring it up at the next family meeting unless it was confidential.

Confidential matters should not be discussed in an open forum. Rather with a one-on-one with the child and both or either parent or someone mature with godly principles they can confide in. The important thing is they release and not harbor bitterness or unanswered questions.

When they ask a question and you do not have an answer, you and the child can pray about that need and later do research or consult someone to find an answer. In the meantime, trust God to give you the revelation to be able to give an answer that is acceptable until you have the fullness of what should be done.

Family meetings also help in preventing family members from having to go outside of the family to acquire the attention or a listening ear they sometimes so desperately need from within the family circle. (See *God's Way and the Blended Family, Chapter Six* for additional information regarding family meetings and communication.)

Please note whether your role model parents are good or poor role models, please realize parents are human. Parents are operating in God-given roles and they will make mistakes. Furthermore, whether they are holy or not, all they can do is the best they know to do, with the knowledge they have at the time they are raising you and your siblings. Pray for them whether they are a good or bad role model and give God space to work in their lives giving them revelation that will improve and enlighten them which will also improve your life.

Everyone should really try to be considerate of one another's space, aware of others bed times and any loud noises. Remember to knock on doors before entering a room and do not borrow anything without permission. This is one example of the kind of information that could be listed in your family guideline.

If the parents have done all they know to do to the best of their ability, knowledge and skills, they can then have a clear conscious even if one or more of their children strayed or became rebellious. After all God the Father is an excellent parent yet many of His children rebelled as well.

People can be attacked in their minds by demonic spirits when they are doing what is right. They are also attacked when they open a door through practicing any type of sin and not repenting. The difference is when you know who you are in Christ you can resist it and be victorious. Knowing meaning it will turn around for your good, Genesis 50:20.

The Bible says when a child does not respect or honor their parents the child runs the risk of shortening their own life but if they show respect they will live long on the earth. Children should obey their parents and adult children should listen to their parent's advice then make the final decision themselves. All ages are to honor and show respect to their parents.

Taken as a whole, realize the parents are still the parents and they should be respected in their home and the parents in turn should give respect to the children. Remember, all of us have *Someone* greater than ourselves or each other to be held accountable to with the responsibilities we have been entrusted to steward over for our household.

Exodus 20:12 KJV says,

> Honour thy father and thy mother: that thy days may belong upon the land which the Lord thy God giveth thee.

Ephesians 6:1-3 KJV says,

> Children, obey your parents in the Lord for this is right. Honour thy father and mother, which is the first commandment with promise; That it may be well with thee, and thou mayest live long on the earth.

Ephesians 6:4 says,

> Fathers do not irritate and provoke your
> children to anger [do not exasperate them
> to resentment], but rear them [tenderly]
> in the training and discipline and the
> counsel and admonition of the Lord.

Everyone is born with a free will. If their choices lead them off the path of righteousness then through our prayers our God will do everything in His power to direct them back into His will simply because He loves them and loves us. He will honor our seed (our child) and prayers according to His Word (Prov. 11:21). Once the Lord shows them the way and makes a way for them they still must decide to follow.

Even though a passage is addressed to the father, whom the responsibility of discipling was given, the mother is to assist the father in the bringing up and teaching of their children, Proverbs 1:8; 6:20.

Psalms 146:8 tells us the Lord opens the eyes of the blind and He lifts up those who are bowed down. He will make the crooked things straight again.

Isaiah 42:16 tells us,

> And I will bring the blind by a way that
> they know not; I will lead them in paths
> that they have not known. I will make

darkness into light before them and make uneven places into a plain. These things I have determined to do [for them]; and I will not leave them forsaken.

The ultimate choice and decision still rests with each individual whether they receive this free gift of love and salvation or not. Therefore, do all you know to do in the sight of God, then pray and leave the battle to Him, 2 Chron. 20:15.

Chapter 4
God's Order, a Higher Lifestyle, and the Purpose for Family Roles

Our God is a God of order. Things just don't happen by chance. There is a purpose for doing things a certain way within a certain time frame that will accomplish or cause you to reach a particular goal. *God works within the order, pattern and timing He sets up.* Our God moves in seasons which involves His perfect timing and His perfect will within a given season. Needless to say, if people are outside of God's will and timing there is a strong possibility they will miss what He has for them at that appointed time. They will need to wait until the door opens again. It is by our choice to be or not to be in a position to receive from Him when it is time for certain promises to manifest in our life.

Being conscious of His divine order and keeping balance in our life is God's will and when we are led by His Spirit, receiving divine wisdom, using discernment and setting proper priorities they will enable us to maintain and have a strong upright, peaceful, joyful and orderly life. Plus stay in His will and timing as much as possible so we can continue to move forward and receive His best for us in that hour.

"Dominion and awe belongs to God; He establishes *order* in the heights of heaven," Job 25:2 NIV. He set up the *order* first in the Heavens the spiritual world then He set up the *order* in our world and delegated it to mankind when He gave us *authority* over all the earth.

Genesis 1:26 tells us,

> God said, Let Us [Father, Son, and Holy Spirit] make mankind in Our image, after Our likeness, *and let them have complete authority...over all the earth...*

As we walk in our authority we have the power to take dominion over all of the earth starting within the framework of God's Order. One of the reasons God established a Family was in order to be their God and for them to be His people. In the next passage, we see within the Family of God, He set up an order.

In Genesis 26:25 it says,

> And [Isaac] **built an altar** there and called on the name of the Lord and **pitched his tent** there; and there Isaac's servants were **digging a well.** (Emphasis added.)

With Isaac God came first. Before doing anything else in the new place, *he built an altar* and then waited there to call upon the Lord. His relationship with God came first with the One Who enabled him with grace to take care of everything else in his life.

He pitched his tent; his home came second. He made provision for his family with a place to live where the family could function and relate to one another. Because he went to God first, God revealed to him the best place for him to settle his family and much more.

His servants dug a well; his business came third. He took care of building his business by giving his servants instructions. He was an entrepreneur.

God's order places people's personal relationships with others and provision for their life as the second most important thing next to their personal relationship with Him. Why? **Because man's relationship with God is his "lifeline" to everything else.**

The Pattern for the Order of Priorities Set in Place by God, is as follows:

> A Personal Relationship with God
> Immediate Family
> Extended Family
> Ministry, Business, Work
> Rest (Trusting God and Physical Rest)
> Recreation

Our God is a relational God. He loves to fellowship, He loves to be with people and He loves to be included. In all He has done and provided, my prayer is we do not forget about Him! And *please notice relationships are placed before* *work.* If relationships are so important to Him then it should be important to us!

In the Kingdom of God in order to really serve/worship God and to keep Him first, not only is a personal relationship with Him necessary but it is required in order to see the fullness of God in your life. It is the complete opposite to what people are accustomed to doing while living a worldly/secular lifestyle (those that are not Born-again Believers). Many things Believers do will not make much sense to someone with a worldly/secular perspective. Looking from the outside in at your personal relationship with God and how you respond to Him and His instructions.

I Cor. 2:14-16 tells us,

> But the natural, nonspiritual man does not accept *or* welcome *or* admit into his heart the gifts *and* teachings, *and* revelations of the Spirit of God, for they are folly (meaningless nonsense) to him; and he is incapable of knowing them [of progressively recognizing, understanding, and becoming better acquainted with them] because they are spiritually discerned *and* estimated *and* appreciated.

> But the spiritual man tries all things [he examines, investigates, inquiries into, questions, and discerns all thing], yet is

himself to be put on trial and judged by no one [he can read the meaning of everything, but no one can properly discern or appraise *or* get an insight into him].

For who has known *or* understood the mind (the counsels and purposes) of the Lord so as to guide *and* instruct Him *and* give Him knowledge? But we have the mind of Christ (the Messiah) *and* do hold the thoughts (feelings and purposes) of His heart.

One of the reasons God should be first, even before family relationships, is so a person will not place anyone or anything before God. If they do that person or thing becomes an idol to them. By keeping Him first, God is in a position in your life to protect all that concerns you. *Therefore, when the Lord is first before your family members it is for their good for He is the only One who can save and help everyone beyond what people can do, Matthew 10:37.*

If you rely on another human being as your main source you are limiting yourself and being unfair to that person because they cannot possibly fill the void or do anything else for your life the way a loving and living God can. Furthermore, if you keep a person first because you are so concerned about them it will turn into worry and fear for their well-being. Fear does not move God's hand, only faith does. The more you try to help others in your own strength the more you are relying on yourself and not on a loving God.

Now because He is first in your life and you have chosen to conform to His example of living He is now in a position where you can cast your care (your burdens) on Him releasing the weight of it and He will sustain you, guide you and take care of whatever concerns you, Psalm 55:22; I Peter 5:7.

All that is needed is to simply keep Him first in your life. One way to continually do that is by reviewing your priorities to make sure God is first before any other person, thing, responsibility or obligation in your daily agenda. *Spend time with Him on a daily basis.* Allow Him through Holy Spirit to guide you, assist and reveal things to you that will change and/or add to your life for your success. Support the Kingdom of God and so forth.

In Matthew 10:33-39 it says,

> But whoever denies *and* disowns Me before men, I also will deny *and* disown him before My Father Who is in heaven… And a man's foes will be they of his own household. He who loves [and takes more pleasure in] father or mother more than [in] Me is not worthy of Me; and he who loves [and takes more pleasure in] son or daughter more than [in] Me is not worthy of Me; And he who does not take up his cross and follow Me

[cleave steadfastly to Me, conforming wholly to My example in living and, if need be, in dying also] is not worthy of Me. **Whoever finds his [lower] life will lose it [the higher life], and whoever loses his [lower] life on My account will find it [the higher life].** (Emphasis added.)

"Jesus' message will not be received by everyone, for the gospel runs at cross purposes with the values and vision of the world. Thus, in some cases it will cause conflict. Its call reverses worldly priorities so that God takes first place even before family relationships. Family members who do not accept Christ's invitation to the cross will fight against those who do. Jesus did not intend to cause conflict, but the natural reaction of the unbeliever is to oppose all who live out Christ's message." [1]

God's order is important to Him. In that order one thing should not be neglected in order to attend to another. He will give you the wisdom on how and when to attend to each, so balance in your life will be maintained.

Rest and recreation are both important in maintaining balance and having godly order in your life as well. Rest for our bodies is extremely important to Almighty God. 3 John 2 says,

"Beloved, I pray that you may prosper in every way and [that your body] may keep well…" Jesus paid a dear price for us to be redeemed, heal and whole. Therefore, if you are a child of God He has chosen our body to be a temple for His Spirit to dwell in while we are on this earth. So, taking care of it with proper food, rest, working conditions and so on pleases God for it shows honor to Him by honoring what He gave us and taking care of it so He can use it for His Glory.

What is the Higher Life as Opposed to the Lower Life?

Because you are striving to live in His order by keeping Him first you will experience the Higher Life.

Let's begin with the lower life. It is a carnal, in the natural, secular life one lives day in and day out without much purpose, toward a destiny or with future plans. Only their own natural self-centered motives drive them to go forward with their regular routine of life such as: going to work, going to school, going to weddings, funerals, holiday events, endless traveling and so forth. Basing their happiness on their circumstances alone. Living basically a defeated life because a real successful life is in Christ in His will or plan for your life.

God measures success differently from the way man does who primarily only bases success on how much material gain he has acquired in life. *There is nothing wrong with wealth and material resources, real or personal properties, but if that is all you have to show for your life you are falling short and don't even know it. "For what does it profit a man to gain the whole world, and forfeit his life [in the eternal Kingdom of God]?"* Mark 8:36.

The lower life can be a complicated one because basically without God in it people are usually selfish and self-centered; frustrated; living in and with their various sins; emotionally and/or physically in pain with no real answers or godly role models in their lives. They are also usually: feeling condemned; feeling guilty about something; living with unforgiveness and bitterness about what someone did to them or the life they have.

Additionally, having shame about some event that happened and living in lack (poverty or with a poverty mentality even if they have money or resources). The lower life also includes being angry, in fear and not in faith, jealous and envious when they compare themselves to others because they do not know what their purpose in life is. They are in broken relationships or relationships that are in the process of falling apart primarily because other people cannot give you what you need to fill that void in your gut or heart.

There is not much hope for the future, everything seems routine and they question, "Is this all there is to life?" *This is a picture of the lower life and when you in your best efforts try to save yourself and make positive changes to obtain the higher life you only continue in your present lifestyle because the higher life is only obtainable one way.*

The Lord said "whoever loses his [lower] life on My account will find it [the higher life]." *So, what exactly is the higher life?* The higher life begins by receiving Jesus Christ as your Lord and Savior. From there you become a new person on the inside and start to develop in His love and grace as you renew your mind in the things of God and follow His ways which is a process that is learned, Romans 12:1-2. You are entitled to live in His promises which are many good things you cannot even imagine, Ephesians 3:20. You live your dream. Once you learn the process of how to live a life in the Kingdom of God you will find it is not one full of *inner turmoil*, strife or confusion but it can be an exciting life.

There is peace, joy, righteousness and little effort to sustain contentment as you continue to move higher in the things of God and with natural resources and abundance. With God *you acquire favor* in your life which brings restoration, assistance, promotion, supernatural increase, honor, real estate and money without sorrow, recognition, victories, policies changed for your good, and so on.

You also have a life of good relationships that are divinely inspired and connected with you; a heart to give and help others instead of being selfish; health and the power to be healed; forgiveness and more able to forgive others rather than live a life full of unforgiveness and bitterness. Also, receiving and living in "The Blessing" of God with the inheritance He has for each one of His children.

Worshipping a faithful and true God is a privilege. Not everyone is blessed to have a living and loving God in their life that speaks to them and answers their prayers. *Believers* are blessed to have true love, patience and endurance with strength to follow through and a mind free from torment as they follow the instructions written in His Word (the Bible).

With this life also comes an inner joy, something not based on outward circumstances to make you happy but a real joy in your heart that gives you hope and strength to go on. A joy that will enable you to see things from a good perspective. With the higher life you also have the authority given to you in the name of Jesus to remove evil strongholds from your life and the lives of your family, friends or whosoever the Lord directs you to.

In addition, to your family you will inherit a new family, a Spiritual Family of like-minded believing people, not perfect people but people who have the same goal to live and follow Jesus' example to the best of their ability. You also have the privilege of fellowshipping or visiting with them on a regular weekly basis in an atmosphere of worship, praise and thanksgiving.

There is so much more to the higher life that it all cannot possibly be explained and for some it will be an unrealistic lifestyle. But the Word of God promises these things and more. Many have already obtained them. The Word also says for those who live in the lower life they will see the higher life as foolishness (I Corinthians 2:14) and something that is unobtainable, a fantasy life and not realistic.

But I assure you it is a very real way of living and it is very easily obtainable and the Comforter (Holy Spirit) will enable you with His grace (power) to maintain and live it every day of your life.

Roles Assist Us on How to Function in Everyday Life

There is no such thing as a role-less marriage or family and when it is attempted you will discover chaos, resentment and strife will occur. You will find much is left for assumption and not enough has been defined, people in the family are not clear as to what is expected of them and many will assume someone else will take care of "it."

The ones who are energized will pick up the slack too often for the ones who are passive or lazy. This situation can only lead to major problems as burn out begins to set in and resentment starts to occur. Complete disorder is not godly, therefore if God is not in it then your flesh and/or Satan is.

Some members of a family may view roles as confining, putting people in a box, and limiting people and their choices. Also, if traditional roles are forced on family members and they become locked into a role without any compromises, compensation or flexibility this may lead to rebellion or withdrawal later.

The biblical roles would be the wiser ones to function in. In considering roles, take into consideration what feels right in your heart, who has the interest, the time and other factors that could play a part in deciding a particular role since functions are attached to all roles. As opposed to traditional roles which may be cut and dry and assigned to a certain gender because it is traditional. *Biblical roles may or may not assign functions that seem right to secular (worldly) people or to even a "religious" person for that matter.*

However, if it is right in the Believer's heart the one who is following the leading of the Holy Spirit and they have a complete peace and probably confirmation about it, then it is right before God and is what matters.

The biblical role addresses one's responsibility not the status of their importance. One role is not better or superior to another making someone else's role inferior. Their roles are just different from one another.

The roles between a husband and wife are equal in value and importance. They are not meant to be the same but used to help and complement the other, in other words their role helps to complete the other.

The biblical marriage and roles of the husband and wife are patterned after Christ's marriage to the church. Both of their roles include loving one another, with a motive and heart to work together for the good of their family. **They can develop from and bring balance into their roles if they keep the right perspective and motive in their hearts.**

Functioning *first* unto God and not just to seek approval from each other, extended family members, friends, neighbors or even their children is wise. In other words what we do, we do with God in mind seeking to please Him first before pleasing anyone else. Why? Because the desire to please God first keeps things in perspective and it acknowledges and thanks Him for being the One Who gave you the health, the mind, wisdom, provision, family and home in the first place. If you are not looking to be affirmed by people it will also prevent you from feeling like others are taking you for granted when they are not appreciative.

The couple should strive in their daily routine, to bring as much beauty and love into their home as possible by letting the light of God shine through them as they endeavor to complete their responsibilities. *As parents we must realize we symbolically represent God's character to our children.* When parents are doing their best and their children reject them, the children are not only in disobedience to their parents but they are also rejecting God's established order for family life Deut. 21:18-21.

Parents should speak freely about the Lord in their home. Their children should see them reading and honoring His Holy Word (separately or together). Let their children see them praying together for the family and other people's needs. Let the children see them fellowshipping in their home with other like-minded people and let them see them attempting to live up-right. If the parents make a mistake let their children see them ask for forgiveness, repent and continue to trust and rely on their faith in God's trusted Word.

Let their children see their parents being kind to one another; complimenting each other; making decisions together. And let them see you Mom honoring, respecting and listening to your husband. Let them see you Dad loving and being considerate to your wife paying attention to her input and her needs. Children of all ages should see a strong bond between their parents. Parents who have learned to yield to the Holy Spirit and who desire to spend time together and time with their family.

Their roles should also include praying for each other, forgiving on a daily basis, communicating at meals or touching bases when they are apart during the day. As they complete their daily tasks with integrity and the right frame of mind it helps to build trust and security in the relationships of family members. It keeps harmony in the home and fills the atmosphere with love and respect for their family and for God. *People of integrity* are preserved, protected, promoted and vindicated according to the Word of God because it keeps you in right standing, Eph. 6:14; Ps 26:1; Ps 25:21; Ps 41:12; Prov.11:3; Prov.19:1; Prov. 20:7.

Many women do not feel appreciated because their husbands and children may not say a simple thank you while they live in a clean and organized home, have decent and healthy meals to eat, clean clothes to wear, have prayer coverage from Dad's and Mom's prayers and Mom's encouraging words for the day. Not to mention they do not have to come home to find their Mother involved in things that would embarrass the family.

It is the little things Mother's do that are taken for granted and if they were not done the family could not function without chaos. If her husband hasn't enough time to completely fill-in or if she is a single mom then she may be stretched to the max. Some households would probably resort to functioning on a one-on-one basis, it's everyone for themselves or the older kids helping the younger or the younger pulling their own weight.

Roles give each person an opportunity to know what is expected of them. The Mother is the heart of the home and it is her responsibility along with the support of her husband to see it runs smoothly. Responsibilities within a role can change rather easily and appropriately when the interest and abilities of an individual changes and it is agreed the change is for the well-being of the family. Changes and modifications of responsibilities within a role could be expressed at a family meeting. Avoid moving in someone else's role. Keep everything decent and in order so everyone has a peace about their role and what is expected of them in their family home.

Chapter 5
Biblical Instructions for the Role of the Husband

In setting up roles in a family and delegating authority, God has designated the husband as the head of his home. The Word says, in Ephesians 5:23 "For the husband is the head of the wife as Christ is the Head of the church…" The passage in Ephesians 5:21-33 is referring to the similarity of how Jesus led the church as an analogy of how a husband is to lead his wife as the head of his family as Jesus is the Head of the Church. Jesus always kept His purpose and assignment in mind and stayed focused for the good of His bride.

Therefore, Jesus is the biblical and prime role model for any man who is serious about being the head of his home in a godly manner. Keep in mind the man that is a Born-again Christian, filled with the Infilling of the Holy Spirit, devoted to studying the Word of God to better equip himself, to follow biblical instructions, not even he could do what Jesus did perfectly. *Because there are no perfect people.* But with the grace of God he would have the wisdom, ability and favor to do so in an excellent manner as opposed to someone trying to lead in his own strength without the knowledge, wisdom and strength of God.

Being the head is not speaking about male dominance or about forcing ungodly ways on his wife and children. Many men have been misinformed and given the wrong information regarding being the head of a household. He is not a god in his house. Many men are following practices God did not intend to be followed in the treatment of their wives.

Being the head means he is to love his wife and children, take care of them, provide for them and protect them. In other words, he is responsible for his wife and children in a domestic setting.

Our example is Jesus. At the time He was on the earth, incarnate, He knew how to be a true Leader and Head. Someone Who was not afraid of responsibility and confrontation. Yet He was there to support and be of service to the church (the people) as He ministered Father God's truths, healed the sick and raised the dead.

In other words, Jesus did not lord over the people, He let them come to Him freely because there is liberty in Christ. He was just and did His share. He laid His life down for those He loved. *He is the King of kings yet, He was humble enough to become a servant and wash the feet of His disciples.* He was supportive and loved to have children around Him. He also loved to see justice and was yielded to the Father Himself.

Jesus is also a gentleman, one that is confident, forgiving and is faithful. He extends grace to all who will receive it. He is powerful, an excellent protector, an awesome businessman, and He gives unconditional love to His family and to those not of His family. He keeps His Word and does not break any of His promises, shows mercy, is upright and full of righteousness. He looks forward to fellowshipping with those in His family, loves justice, and said He would never leave us nor forsake us. (See *God's Way and Knowing the King* for additional information regarding Jesus/Yeshua the Anointed One.)

A Husband, the Head of His Home God's Way

The only way to be the head of your home is to seek God first. As a Christian man, he is to participate with his wife and children and usher in God's presence. Pray for his family daily. He is to be an example, and a good role model for his children. Discuss the Word of God with his family especially in areas of God's grace, faith, mercy, salvation, forgiveness, obedience to God's Word, finances, health/healing and other subjects found in the Word. The Word of God speaks about any subject pertaining to life.

When your household is a Family of God every member is a priest and king regardless of gender, race or status. Corporately we are all kings and priest if we are in the Body of Christ, Revelation 1:5-6; I Peter 2:5, 9.

The Only High Priest is the Messiah, Hebrews 4:15 tells us,

> For we do not have a High Priest Who is unable to understand *and* sympathize *and* have a shared feeling with our weaknesses *and* infirmities *and* liability to the assaults of temptation, but One Who has been tempted in every respect as we are, yet without sinning.

Jesus is the High Priest of all families that receive Him as their Lord and Savior. All authority in heaven and on earth was given to Jesus and His Words are Spirit and Life, Matthew 28:18; John 6:63. *God is the final authority.*

Therefore, *a man is not the spiritual head or final authority.* A man would only be the natural head of his family. And the only one with authority to tell a Christian wife when and if she can read the Bible, or whether or not she can attend church or tithe or teach the Word of God or participate in helping others as she is led by Holy Spirit, is the High Priest of their home and that is Christ Jesus, the Messiah. God is the only One who calls, anoints and sends forth a person (male or female) to do a work for Him.

Ephesians 5:23, 25 NIV Briefly Speaks to this Issue,

> For the husband is the head of the wife as Christ is the head of the church, his body, of which he is the Savior. Husbands, love your wives, just as Christ loved the church and gave Himself up for her…

The husband is the head of the wife as Christ the Messiah is the head of the church. The church consists of male and female. Therefore, the husband God is speaking to is a saved man, a Believer. This instruction is for a husband that is a Believer and is the head of his household. As his example, Christ, is the head of the church.

If the man is not saved (a born-again Believer) then it would be difficult for Him to love his wife as Christ loved the church. If he is not in the Family of God and has a personal relationship with God, then he does not know Him. (See *God's Way and Knowing the King* for information on developing a personal relationship with God.)

This is why it is important for a couple to be equally yoked. When both are saved (Believers) they have received the same Lord and Savior to worship, fellowship with and is a part of their marriage covenant. It is not good to be unequally yoked (married to an unbeliever) 2 Cor. 6:14.

However, if you are married to an unbeliever and desire to stay that is fine, the marriage is sanctified because of you (whether the saved person is a man or woman). However, if the unbeliever chooses to leave then let them go, I Corinthians 7:15. God does not go against a person's will because each of us has been given a free will to choose Deut. 30:19.

The Father's Presence in the Home is Extremely Important

The father's presence is extremely important to validate and affirm his wife and children. He is the source and sustainer, the head, the protector, teacher, leader, primary one that disciplines, he is a nurturer, and he is the very foundation of his family.

When a father speaks his voice usually commands a certain amount of respect and not out of fear but a reverence for his position in the family. This position was given to him by God and we are to respect God's order.

One way he nurtures his family is to become the source and sustainer as the provider who receives his instructions and resources from his Maker as he yields to God's will for his life.

A man's wife was never intended to replace him but to help and assist him in his functions and endeavors to achieve the desired results and goals set-up by God. These goals pertain to his primary role in life as a *family man regardless of any other endeavors.*

The husband is not to relinquish his duty to nurture his children in the faith. Therefore, if he is not familiar with God's Word or desires for his family to be exposed to more than he and his wife's teachings of the Word, they can also attend Bible study at their local Word church. If they do not have a local church then a good home Bible study can work to.

There are also Christian television and internet programs available where the entire family can learn and enjoy the Word together at home. In addition, there are thousands of resources available to purchase through Christian bookstores, ministries, other online book and product distributors, as well as Amazon.

There are also ministry conferences and events that would give he and his family a strong foundation in the Word of God. The family could benefit from all of these resources that would enable them to enjoy a successful and prosperous life. The only condition would be to follow the leading of the Holy Spirit for the teaching vehicles best for their family.

In Ephesians 6:4 it says,

> Fathers, do not irritate and provoke your
> children to anger [do not exasperate them
> to resentment], but rear them [tenderly]
> in the training and discipline and the
> counsel and admonition of the Lord.

When fathers simply follow the teachings of Jesus and are led by Holy Spirit they will have the wisdom to lead their household. They will know how to be a fair and loving parent to their children. Therefore, their children will have no reason to be irritated or provoked by them.

Granted many times a father must say no to certain things their children cannot participate in or have but *if an explanation is included* for understanding their decision that should be sufficient. His children will grow to understand the decision they thought was unfair or unreasonable was really in their best interest and for their good.

Fathers who are tender with their sons will raise true men. Society teaches fathers to be abrupt and harsh with their sons thinking it will make them hard and manly but God's ways are different and work better.

Teach them the Word of God, show them love, follow through with your word, teach them with discipline, know how to say you are sorry when you are wrong, love and respect their mother and give them time in your busy schedule. When you have a number of children it is best not to show favoritism but treat them all with the same respect and integrity. (See *God's Way and the Blended Family, Chapter Four* for information regarding the difference between discipline and punishment in training up children.)

His Wife According to the Bible is Versed, Permitted and Equipped to Assist

His wife is called to assist her husband teach and train up their children in the Word of God as a part of her role as his wife, Prov. 31:15, 26, 28.

His wife's teaching can also extend to their local church and beyond as she is equipped by God to minister the Word. *However,* **some men have been taught "all women" in regard to teaching the Word of God are to be quiet in the church** *and certainly when it comes to teaching men from the Bible.*

One of the Scriptures Used Out of Context to Support this View is, I Timothy 2:11-15a,

Let a woman learn in quietness, in entire submissiveness. I allow no woman to teach or to have authority over men; she is to remain in quietness and keep silence [in religious assemblies] …

It is time for the men and women who are in bondage in this area to be set free and come up higher in the things of God in order to receive all God has for them. This would include a help meet who is free to fulfill the mandate God set in order so she can operate and be in agreement with her husband. This will release the dominion (complete authority) over the territory God gave them which would include but is not limited to their home, Gen. 1:26-28.

Concerning the above passage, I Tim. 2:11-15a, Apostle Paul wrote this to accommodate the people he was ministering to. He had to relate to them based on their education, where they were spiritually as well as the place and time they lived in.

Further Explanation of Paul's Message [1]

> *The ultimate restoration of that regrettable situation (the unnamed woman in I Timothy 2:11-15a)* **was not to ban all women from public ministry.** No. Instead, in I Timothy 3:11 which says, "[The] women likewise must be worthy of respect and serious, not gossipers, but temperate and self-controlled, [thoroughly] trustworthy in all things*;"* *Paul was stating the qualities necessary for godly women to be released into public ministry.* This is exactly the same thing Paul did to counter the harmful influence of the men who were promoting heresy—Hymenaeus and Alexander (I Tim. 1:20). **Just because these two men misused their teaching gifts, Paul didn't eliminate all men from roles of leadership.** No, to prevent further problems, he likewise set down

guidelines for men leaders (I Tim. 3:2-10, 12-13). Thus, we see that **Paul dealt with men and women evenhandedly, correcting those of both genders who fell into heresy**, instructing men and women in the ways of spiritual leadership so that they would not "fall into disgrace and the devil's trap" (I Tim. 3:7).

Are the women of verse 11 deacons or the wives of deacons? The structure of the letter and the content of Paul's message suggest that Paul fully intended women to serve in the leadership of the church. After all, hadn't *Paul begun the ministry in this city with Priscilla and her husband, Aquila? Nowhere in his writings do we see Paul withholding leadership responsibilities from godly women.* On the contrary, we know from his comments concerning Phoebe in Romans 16:1-2 that *he saw her as a fellow servant of the Lord, affirmed her as a deacon, and commended her as an exemplary leader of the church.* (Also see author's addition – Philippians 4:3 where it says, "I exhort you too, [my] genuine yokefellow, help these [two women to keep on cooperating], for they have toiled along with me in [the spreading of] the good news (the

Gospel), as have Clement and the rest of my fellow workers whose names are in the Book of Life."

Paul's word to us is not one that makes harsh divisions between men and women, neither with the way they are saved nor with the way they are released into ministry. On the contrary, before the Cross, the playing field is leveled. If we are to fulfill God's forever dream— reaching everyone with the opportunity to be reconciled to Him, every one of us must pray, profess our faith, and live peaceful and quiet lives. **Every one of us should follow God's leading into whatever ministry He chooses. This is true for men and likewise for women.** (Emphasis Added.)

Another example that comes to mind is the example of *Deborah who was a married woman, her husband's name was Lappidoth. She was also a prophet and she judged Israel,* Judges 4:4. Deborah prophesied to Barak that God had a mission for him and he was to gather 10,000 men to fight in this battle. This man of war told the prophetess, "If you will go with me, then I will go; but if you will not go with me, I will not go. And she said, I will surely go with you…" Judges 4:6-8.

This man knew that he needed the help of the Lord and he recognized she was appointed as a prophet and a judge over Israel (the same offices Samuel the prophet held). Deborah could not have walked in the offices of prophet and judge without having been anointed and appointed with assignments from Almighty God.

Barak further humbled himself knowing the glory would not go to him but to a woman, Judges 4:9; 22. This man understood it was God's battle. Therefore, he let go of all pride to seize the victory that was assured if the prophetess was with him with the presence of God and to give further instructions if needed. (In the Old Testament God only spoke through the prophets, priest and the kings).

God's thoughts and ways are higher than those of men, (Isa. 55:9) and we would all see more victories in our lives if we would simply yield to His ways. "...Believe in the Lord your God and you shall be established; believe and remain steadfast to His prophets and you shall prosper," regardless of whether the prophet is a male or female 2 Chronicles 20:20b.

In addition, the scripture I Timothy 2:11-15a and others like it have been taken out of context and used to silence the female from her God-given purpose, assignments, rights and role as a person or minister of God. If there were no other examples showing God did indeed use women to teach from the Bible then, so be it, but since there are numerous examples of God using women not only to teach but as a leader in His Kingdom, a person's interpretation of the scriptures are invalid and have no authority in this area because the Greater Authority has already spoken, Matthew 28:18.

The Christian husband is to oversee or supervise his home by keeping himself in line with God's Word. He is to keep all demonic strongholds out and doors closed that evil forces would try to come through to attack his family. When he is not in his set place or doing what God told him to do he has opened a door for spiritual attacks which will manifest in his natural life. He is responsible to keep a hedge of protection around his home by decreeing and speaking life to his family and situation.

He should be declaring the blood of Jesus and literally putting on the whole armor of God daily as well as living upright while keeping himself pure before God as he continues to develop in his personal relationship with the Lord.

*And above all he is to fully understand **Jesus is the High Priest** Who has been given all authority in heaven and on earth* (Hebrews 4:15; Matt. 28:18) and as a son and a priest he is to look to Father God in the name of Jesus and in the power of the Holy Spirit for his help, wisdom, protection, guidance and provision.

Even though the husband is the primary provider (he may not be the only provider for the home). This includes where the family lives, provisions for food, clothing and things to keep the family intact and comfortable for daily living.

Furthermore, he is to *cast his care and concerns to God, be flexible,* be responsible to do what he knows and has the ability to do expecting

God's wisdom and help to sustain his family. He should expect God to give him instructions, directions, connections, a means to provide and miracles. Also, an abundance in all areas to maintain what God blessed him with as well as an overflow in order to bless others outside of his home.

A Christian Man's Role According to Titus 2:2; 6-8 says,

Urge the older men to be temperate, venerable (serious), sensible, self-controlled, and sound in the faith, in the love, and in the steadfastness and patience [of Christ]. *In a similar way, urge the younger men to be self-restrained and to behave prudently [taking life seriously].* And show your own self in all respects to be a pattern and a model of good deeds and works, teaching what is unadulterated, showing gravity [having the strictest regard for truth and purity of motive], with dignity and seriousness. And let your instruction be sound and fit and wise and wholesome, vigorous and irrefutable and above censure, so that the opponent may be put to shame, finding nothing discrediting or evil to say about us. (Emphasis added.)

It takes true humility to be the support your partner needs you to be. A husband operating in his biblical role would be very supportive of his wife not taking her role lightly or for granted but understanding her part helps fulfill his. *His wife's part is not inferior to the point where he believes her part in the relationship is unimportant but to simply understand it is different.*

Realizing, if they work together faithfully in their respective roles they will be able to have a peaceful home, and to raise sound, joyful, educated children with godly character who will live within the Kingdom of God yet be ready to function within society as a whole.

Men in general have more responsibilities delegated to them by God. The husband may delegate certain decision making to his wife but certainly not all of it. Major decisions should *not be made without both of them discussing it first.* The two of them should pray and ask for wisdom, direction and be in agreement about major decisions. This would be the proper order, especially for anything major. If there is a problem in making the decision, *the man should make the final decision even if it is to delegate it to his wife.*

He could delegate for various reasons: maybe she has the time for the project; or maybe he liked her idea or strategy better or maybe he is overloaded with other responsibilities or not familiar with the details of this project as his wife is. ***They are a team and this is his option and right as the head to delegate recognizing it is in the complete will of***

God understanding God was the one who sent him an equipped help meet to start with.

If the husband decides to make a decision about a matter his wife should be in agreement as well. *All decisions should be for the betterment of the entire household.* If, however, a decision is made by him that would place his home in any aspect of jeopardy in anyway and his wife is totally against it and not in agreement then the husband needs to yield and seek God for wisdom and direction before doing anything.

But *if he decides to follow through without being in agreement with his wife,* he needs to understand the threefold cord has been broken. He has given space or place for the adversary to operate and the husband should be prepared to deal with the consequences which may affect the entire household.

His wife should release the matter to God and not worry. She is to be prayerful the Lord will send clarity, instructions and whatever else is needed to the both of them regarding the issue. (See *God's Way and Marriage* for information about the threefold cord and the marriage covenant between a husband, a wife and God.)

Ephesians 5:21 the KJV and the Amplified Versions Regarding Submission,

> Submitting yourselves one to another in the fear of God. Be subject to one

another out of reverence for Christ (the Messiah, the Anointed One).

When operating properly in their roles, submitting one to another a husband and wife are held accountable to one another and to the Lord. This also brings security and safety to the relationship.

> Mutual submission based upon shared reverence for Christ as Lord is one of three evidences of the Spirit-filled life... Christians in Ephesus were concerned how Christians were to deal with authority in these social institutions. Paul's position was that authentic faith in Christ will enable believer's to be in submission to one another even though social custom expected submission only of women, children and slaves.[2] Ephesians 5:21

Submitting One to Another is to Honor and Respect Each Other

In addition to being supportive of each other and helping one another develop their dreams, gifts and talents that God placed on the inside them, know *in a man's eyes the respect that he desires is to be accepted, admired and appreciated by his wife.* He also has a great need to be respected and affirmed in his place of work or business. To feel significant is needed as well to keep his self-esteem and self-worth in tack in order to complete his assignment or purpose in life.

What a husband should understand is that a wife and other people can only fill so many of his needs, if at all. When he goes to his source, his Heavenly Father, every need is met and *he can rest in knowing what God has said about him in His Word.*

God's Word is a man's true affirmation and what will make him feel like it is all worth it. His self-worth won't ever have to be low or suffer because he knows his true worth is not measured by what man says a success is but only by what God declares a successful man is. Therefore, he should know who he is in Christ Jesus, the Anointed One.

Many men have been taught and are led to believe they are the head of "every woman" but that is not what is written by God. *A man is the head of his own wife, Ephesians 5:23.* If a man were the head of every woman then a man could never have a female employer, supervisor, manager or be comfortable listening to a female judge, teacher, general, doctor, minister, police officer and so forth without being in violation of God's Word. He would always have to be in charge over a woman even if he lacked the education, experience, skills, money, connections in a particular work place or in society.

Furthermore, this means any man would be over another man's wife. Think about it, that is only asking for problems and is dangerous primarily because it is not what God said. This would only open a door to destruction. The Word of God made it very clear, a man is *over his own wife.*

God has appointed the male as the head of his house regardless of his education, experience, skills in the work place or salary. These are not the most important things in the domestic setting. The man is to be honored and respected in his house as the head of his family in order for his family to function, to be in obedience and under the protection of Almighty God Who is a God of order and the head of the husband, *Ephesians 5:23.* Whatever is out of order cannot and will not stand.

During the days when Jesus walked the earth the Greek language was the common language was used at that time. In Greek, the word for *wife* was also the same word for *woman.* It was translated into the English version of the Bible as woman and not wife. This caused more confusion and inaccurate teaching on the subject because wives were women but not all women were married and called wives.

Therefore, many misconceptions, confusion and lies are being exposed to bring the man and woman into proper alignment so they can together take dominion and accomplish in the earth God's will for the End-times.

When the husband stands in his place as head and is doing all he knows to do unto God, coupled with praying in God's will, not only will his prayers not be hindered, but God will give him the wisdom and all he will need to be the priest, husband, father, provider, friend, leader and a man of humility for his home. Someone who is not afraid of his responsibilities and secure enough to delegate. He will also respect, listen and seriously consider his wife's opinion and ideas just as he desires his wife to respect his.

I'm sorry to say, so many men feel they must carry on and do it all alone even though he has help at his disposal. Erroneous teaching says, since he is the head, the provider and so forth, he is there to make it comfortable for his wife and family. This would include him keeping all of the problems that come into *their* home to himself to spare his "poor little weak wife the burden."

This kind of thinking is what sends men to an early grave because it is not the will of the Lord. God sent the man capable help to be of assistance to him and a partner to love, if he found the "right wife" according to the Bible. The Word says, "He who finds a [true] wife finds a good thing and obtains favor from the Lord," Proverbs 18:22; 19:14; 31:10.

Even though God has built into women in general many attributes to be a help meet the Proverbs 31 woman has a different anointing to do even more and beyond in a more excellent way. But instead some men believe the lie was sent straight from the pit to deceive him into missing what God gave him as a gift to make his life easier, better and more effective in the natural and spiritual realms.

A part of the untruth, the fabrication that belittles women and destroys marriages is *some men see women as the weaker vessel in "every area" of her existence and so they treat her as a lesser human being.* This makes it difficult for him to see her as a significant other or help meet. It is not necessary for a woman to have large muscles and a great deal of upper body strength (although some female body builders do) for most of the work she is designed to do because women are nurturers at heart.

Men were given upper body strength because he was *designed* to be the provider. Hunting at one time and still is in many parts of the world one avenue or source for the husband to provide for his family. Also, cultivating the soil and planting in the fields were primary roles for the male. He is also the builder, the protector, the fighter to guard and keep the home and to serve in the military.

His strength is needed for so many important roles for his home and in the work place. His strength was not intended by God to be used to beat and/or threaten his wife and children as some men have done, but to guard, love and as I have said to protect them.

I Peter 3:7 Addresses the Issue of a Woman Being Physically the Weaker,

> In the same way you married men should live considerately with [your wives], with an intelligent recognition [of the marriage relation], honoring the woman **as** [physically] the weaker, but [realizing that you] are joint heirs of the grace

(God's unmerited favor) of life, in order that your prayers may not be hindered and cut off. [Otherwise you cannot pray effectively.] (Emphasis added.)

The scripture says to honor the woman *as* physically the weaker vessel... The fact she does not have a lot of body strength does not mean she is weak in her mind or in her inner being. If God sent your wife He knew what was on the "inside of her" would be beneficial to you.

For example, women have an inner strength to deal with certain problems and issues men tend to ignore and one reason being a woman's brain operates more frequently on both sides so they are better equipped to deal with things that are in great "detail." Whereas this could be more irritating to most men whose brain also operates on both sides but not as frequently so they tend to think more in general terms and would rather not be bothered with too much "detail."

Women have an inner strength to not only carry and birth children men do not have, nor do they need since God has chosen the female for this function. Her inner strength brings about an endurance to withstand and tolerate in order to persevere through certain situations and see it through to completion. Not taking anything away from the man they can certainly follow through to completion, however, understand a woman can follow through and endure as well.

Remember she was *inside* of a man, a part of him in the form of his rib or side. Therefore, his support system or helper really came from inside of him demonstrating when God completed His creation mankind was fearfully and wonderfully made, Psalm 139:14. (See *God's Way and Marriage* for additional details regarding the man's rib or side, his support system and helpmeet.)

If a husband does not know the purpose of his wife or what she is capable of nor is he willing to find out because of preconceived ideas of what women can and cannot be or do apart from what God's Word says about them, then more than likely she won't be given the opportunity to work to her fullest potential in their home.

If you do not know the purpose of a wife you will abuse her. This is one reason why some women are labeled aggressive and called all kinds of derogatory names because she in many cases has so much to give and there is no demand for what is on the inside of her or a place to release it.

In most cases she does not fully understand or explain what is inside of her but she knows there is more than what is required or expected. So those women who do step out of the "norm" or stereotype or from under the labels to explore or desire to use the gifts and talents God has placed inside of them are quickly persecuted and made to feel there is something wrong with them or that they are just rebellious.

A word of caution, the scripture I Peter 3:7 clearly states a husband is to honor his wife *as* the physically weaker and remember it has nothing to do with them being joint heirs of the grace of God. Further, the husband can hinder his prayer life which will affect the entire household if he violates the relationship and takes advantage or mistreats his wife because he simply can only see her as a weak vessel and chooses to ignore her inner strength and abilities. *In Genesis 1:26,* ***God gave dominion to the two of you and if you are not in agreement you diminish your God-given authority to have dominion*** *over all of what God gave both of you to have dominion over.*

Furthermore, husbands do not stifle your wife's greatest value to you. Do not make demands of obedience on your wife as if she were a child but with humility and love you are to honor and respect your wife as an equal. Respect her enough to listen and consider her point of view.

In the event, she steps out to assist you, let her know she as a person is valued. Let her know you appreciate her efforts and input. As you affirm her role as your wife and partner in life it will build her confidence and security in the relationship. She will be in a place of peace where she can further hear from the Lord Who will continue to impart wisdom, strength and direction to her. For projects at hand, the Lord will give your wife all that is needed and necessary to fulfill her purpose. As a result, everyone in the home and at the workplace (if she works) will greatly benefit.

Men and Women are Different

God made males and females different and to have different roles and together they make a strong and powerful team to fulfill God's purpose for their lives. *Together honoring, respecting, celebrating and admiring each other's strengths and picking up the slack where there is a weakness they can win in every battle.* **However, when divided, comparing, competing and belittling each other because of their differences and weaknesses they will surely fall.**

"As a society, we've managed to confuse equal *rights* with equal *roles*. We've come to believe, wrongly, that the roles of husband and wife are interchangeable. Guided by this mistaken notion, we've arrived at an erroneous conclusion: that role reversal inside the marriage is not only an acceptable thing but also a desirable thing. We've confused equal treatment *under the law* with equal roles *inside the marriage.* Let me take a moment to make an observation...

Men and Women are different.

Very different.

Not just *physically* different.

Not just *emotionally* different.

Not just *psychologically* different.

Men and women are different in all these ways and more. But modern culture has encouraged us to ignore the differences, with the predictably poor consequences. Husbands and wives have become confused about the roles they're expected to play inside a "modern" relationship. Yet the internal constructs of human nature are not in flux. They were established by our Creator long ago. And, like every other thing that God created, He did it according to His own principles and patterns, irrespective of cultural trends.

So it's time to rethink the institution of marriage, not based upon society's point of view, but upon God's point of view. And it's time to pay particular attention to the God-given personality traits that are as old as *man*kind and *woman*kind." [3]

People enter covenants to fill in that part where there are weaknesses by each offering their strengths to make the covenant strong and workable. The male and female sanctioned together by Almighty God is the strongest covenant there is on the face of the planet.

Also, a man should not avoid his God-given role to honestly love and treat his wife as a part of himself. The Word of God says, "...let each man of you [without exception] love his wife as [being in a sense] his very own self..." Ephesians 5:33. And in addition to this, he will strive to love his wife as Christ loves His own body (His bride, the church). This may be difficult for some men if they do not think well of themselves or feel they have failed as providers for their family. This is why the command from God for everyone to love their neighbor as [you do] yourself is so important Matthew 22:39.

Unless we honestly and in a healthy manner can love ourselves, we are incapable of loving anyone else. *If a man who struggles in this area would believe what the Lord has said about him and how He loves him and made him for Himself to fellowship with; he would be able to compare what God, Someone who cannot lie has said, to the negative things that are sent to his mind or through others by the adversary each and every day.*

Men and women are commanded to cast down the wrong imaginations and thoughts about themselves that are sent to their minds or that others have said and renew their minds in what God has said about them 2 Cor. 10:5 KJV and Romans 12:2.

If God the Father thought you were worth dying for, enough to send His only begotten Son, at least you can find out why He felt this way by taking the time to search it out in the Word of God for yourself. Simply with a sincere heart, repent for believing the lie about yourself and make a decision to follow truth. Once this is resolved the husband will find it easier to love and cherish his wife as Christ loved and cherished the church. He will also be more content in life and open to find and fulfill his purpose.

Husbands that Desire a Blissfully Happy Home

Husbands please realize when your wife is flourishing and being all God called her to be, she becomes a reflection of her husband's glory. It is the praises of her husband, Prov. 31:28, his choosing to support her with her hearts desires that line up with the Word of God; his choosing to be a protector of his home and stepping up as the leader and head God called him to be will cause her to be a light of her husband's glory.

Proverbs 31:23 says this about this type of woman's husband, "Her husband is respected at the city gate, where he takes his seat among the elders of the land." In other words, he is respected in business and other arenas for using wisdom in making important and sound decisions that affects others' lives.

In addition, because of the joy and contentment in your marital relationship the glory of God will be seen. Furthermore, when you choose to deepen your relationship with your spouse God will broaden your ministry. Your ministry is basically what God purposed for you to do in this life. It is whatever and wherever God put your hands to work. Whether it is a business, in the workplace, in a sanctuary or wherever, God will cause your light, His glory to be upon your life with great favor, Proverbs 18:22; Rev. 19:1; 2 Cor. 4:6; Romans 8:17; Eph. 3:21.

All of the above, along with the other information in this book and God's Word will cause you to have the blissfully happy and wonderful home you hoped for and desired.

Chapter 6
Biblical Instructions for the Role of the Wife

Since God is the creator of marriage and is the author of all roles and functions within a family, it will be to the wife's benefit and advantage to find out what He says a wife's role should be. One pleasing to Him and helpful for she and for the family He so graciously blessed her with.

Therefore, I prefer to follow the biblical definition of what a wife's role is because I have full confidence in God's Word. He can back-up every single Word that is written and none shall return to Him void, Isaiah 55:11.

In order to fulfill her role, she must have the wisdom of God to be creative, active, loving, understanding, humble, dynamic, submissive, and operating many times in the background without any recognition except that which comes from God. Also, she can be fulfilled with the satisfaction of knowing that decent, loving, kind and god-fearing human beings were being developed for a successful and prosperous life's journey and for generations to come.

Before you become a wife, if that is your desire, you should first be whole, confident, content as a woman and focused on a journey fulfilling your true purpose in life. If you do not know your own purpose how will you expect your husband to know and be supportive? If you are a Christian and you have low self-esteem, feel unworthy, insecure or inferior you will need to renew your mind and acquire the understanding of who you are in Christ, the Anointed One, Romans 12:2; I Cor. 2:16; Rom. 8:2; Phil. 2:5; Eph. 2:5; Rom.5:17; Rom. 8:17; 2 Cor. 5:20; 2 Cor. 5:21.

These are only a few of the scriptures that tell you who you are in Christ. Read the Word for yourself and discover the revelation of what is said about a Child of God. You can also see chapter ten which has more of the benefits of being a born-again Christian Believer.

As you seek God in prayer simply ask Him what is your purpose and/or assignment? Pray and read His Word in areas you need answers. By praying and reading His Word it will build you up spiritually as well as strengthen you as you learn His will for your life.

The Lord may or may not answer you with words, it depends on how He communicates with you. But He will place a desire in your heart that will lead you to certain materials to read, listen to or attend meetings or classes that will begin to equip you for your true purpose. He will also begin to show you your gifts and talents (if you are not already aware of them) and elaborate on them. In addition, He will give you favor and open doors to make the right connections for you.

Being sensitive to His Spirit will definitely help you to find the right path and connect with the right people including the right husband for you if you have not yet married. This strategy will also aid if you are already married and are still struggling with the same issues and not obtaining answers and results.

The Wife's Role is Significant for the Well-being of Her Family

Her role centers more on her capacity to *nurture* and be *a helper. A helper is not an inferior role but rather describes a "function" and not "worth."* A wife's highest priority is her family and home. The Bible says, "the older women are to give good counsel and be teachers of what is right and noble, so that they will wisely train the young women to be temperate and disciplined and to love their husbands and their children."

They are to teach them "to be self-controlled, chaste, homemakers, good-natured, (kindhearted), adapting and subordinating themselves to their husbands, that the Word of God may not be exposed to reproach," Titus 2:3-5 paraphrased.

The Bible says, "She rises while it is yet night and gets *[spiritual] food* for her household and assigns her maids their task." In other words, early in the morning she spends time in prayer to receive wisdom and instructions from God and she prepares to delegate work to others for the day, Proverbs 31:15.

It is in those early hours God so graciously will pour out to her all that she needs for that day. He gives you enough grace (enablement) for each day, Phil. 4:13. The wisdom and strength she will need can all be found in His Word. For those of you who are not early risers but prefer to stay up late seek Him before going to sleep and during the quiet moments of your day (if you can't find a moment then make time for Him in your schedule) and as you spend time fellowshipping with Him, He will refresh and energize you when you enter into His presence with singing, praying or reading His Word. You can gain wisdom, strength, peace, strategies, instructions, guidance, and encouragement.

Also, a married woman's role is to work alongside her husband for the betterment of their family. Working unto God and being content and at peace in what she does in the home, with a humble servant-like attitude (a servant's heart) to be of service and assist wherever the help is needed.

The Bible Clearly Informs a Wife How to Love Her Husband in the Eyes of God, Ephesians 5:33 says,

> ...And let the wife see that she respects and reverences her husband [that she notices him, regards him, honors him, prefers him, venerates, and esteems him; and that she defers to him, praises him, and loves and admires him exceedingly].

The Importance of a Help Meet

I shared the importance and function of a helpmeet in *God's Way and Marriage*, however, I felt it needed to be reiterated:

One of the things God says a married woman is, is a helper meet (help meet; helpmate). She is someone who is suitable for her husband, adapted, and complementary to her mate, Genesis 2:20. She is one who is capable and equipped and is sent by God with wisdom, knowledge, gifts and skills to assist her husband. She is her husband's confidante, encourager, spiritual partner, an inward strength and comforter; she is his "helper."

I like to say she is in excellent company because one of the names or attributes of **Holy Spirit is "Helper,"** Hebrews 13:6 and John 16:7. In Psalm 121:2 it says, "My help comes from the Lord, Who made heaven and earth." Here He describes Himself as the "Helper" as well.

Helper in Hebrew is Ezer and is a warfare word. The bride is also a warrior; she is a warrior bride! The bride is called to be a suitable helper to stand side by side with her husband in the battles of life and win. She is sent by God to help her husband fulfill his purpose and vision. She is a *Helper!*

Also, the word "helps" is sunantilambanomai in the original Greek text. It means "to take hold together against." Now, "together" means our participation is required. The Holy Spirit takes "hold together" with us against the problem.

In addition, God in all His power was still humble (Phil. 2:8-9) enough to be called a *Helper* and has placed *the wife* in a similar position on the earth in the most important institution known to mankind, "Marriage and Family."

She is supportive of her husband as he is supportive of her. She submits to her husband and he submits to her. Again, as was stated in the Biblical Instructions in the Role of the Husband chapter, it says in Ephesians 5:21 KJV, ***"Submitting yourselves one to another in the fear of God"*** is accomplished as they honor and respect one another. This includes being supportive of each other by helping one another develop the dreams, gifts and talents God placed on the inside of each of them.

One way to accomplish this is to adapt, make adjustments, compromise, be flexible and not try to change your spouse to fit into what you think they should be but to help your spouse become all God has called them to be by helping them develop their potential, gifts, talents and skills through your prayers.

With wisdom and knowledge ladies, ***you are equipped as a helper to use your God-given skills for daily tasks which are not limited to*** running the affairs of your household. Things such as being a mother; planning and preparing meals; managing the household spending plan; shopping; organizing schedules; working; planning and executing family functions and events; date nights; doing laundry; cleaning and sorting; dropping-off and picking-up children for school and activities; supervising school homework; using great ideas and giving suggestions and information.

Also, *delegating* to a housekeeper, chef, tutors, family members or staff as you complete as much of your daily agenda and goals as time allows. Trying to maintain balance and rest in between responsibilities or projects as you move forward to completion. These are only a portion of the functions with more on the nurturing end which wives are called, anointed and equipped by God to do.

In helping her husband fulfill the vision and purpose for his life which will ultimately affect their entire household. If he is with the wife God has chosen for him, his wife will understand and be supportive of the vision because the Lord will give it to her as well so she can embrace it and be supportive.

Therefore, the vision, goals and dreams in their hearts will give them the true purpose and ministry God has for them together. And many times, it is a family vision with generational blessings attached to it. Their purpose will ultimately be used to help maintain the marriage and family ties, as the adversary will do all in his power to try and stop it from coming to fruition. And many times, the only way to stop the couple's vision or dream from manifesting is to stop them by attacking their marriage.

Ask God for wisdom, instructions and guidance in "helping your husband." Either spouse could ask the other how they could assist in helping where it is needed. However, most men do not think they need a "helper." Most see themselves as the helpers and not needing the help.

Because they see themselves as the helpers, as independent operators and problem solvers, decision makers and so forth they may not respond well to their wife's "*help.*" God was the One who said in Genesis 2:18 "It is not good for man to be alone." The woman did not say this the Creator said it. He said the man needed a helpmate. So, God gives Him a wife who is suitable and capable to help him achieve his goals, to help fight the battles of life and to help run his household in a smooth and orderly manner.

But because the man and woman don't fully understand what God has placed inside of them there is conflict, misunderstandings and wrong conceptions when she tries to help. As the man disregards the implied warning in Genesis chapter two and overlooks the fact God has appointed a wife to help him there will be continuous struggles.

> A woman's desire to support her husband is simply a manifestation of her God-given nature as a helpmate. Our wives were created with a natural need to secure, protect, correct, and give advice whether we men want it or not. In fact, the number one complaint that men have about women is that women are always trying to control them... A woman's questions (which is harmless to her) may

be interpreted by her man as meddling. What to a woman seems helpful advice can be interpreted by the man as a threat to his authority. What to a woman seems "assisting" is often viewed by the man as "controlling" A woman's subtle hint can be easily misinterpreted by her man as nagging. But that's usually not how she meant it at all.

Until men understand that their wives have an internal need to help –and until wives begin to understand that their husbands have a built-in "control-detector" – communication inside the marriage will suffer... If Husbands and wives understand two important facts: first, that God created women with an inborn need to help, and second, that men need the help women were created to give.[2]

I believe God knows best and if we trust Him He will help both the man and the woman understand each other better. They would be able to discern and see the true motives and the heart of their spouse. As we follow the leading of Holy Spirit and His Word concerning marital issues and not allow pride but humility to operate we will have the victory that is promised.

Another Key Function of a Wife is to be Her Husband's Spiritual Partner

A wife is to share in the spiritual development, discipline, structure, guidelines and so on as a part of the upbringing of their children. To confirm the Lord would have *both parents* teach their children His will from His written Word, He says to the child, "My son, hear the instruction of your father; reject not nor forsake the teaching of your mother" Proverbs 1:8; Proverbs 6:20.

God entrusted women to be the first to spread the Good News of the Gospel, that Jesus had risen from the grave. Thereby entrusting women to take instructions, obey and follow through with the Word of God, Matthew 28:5-10. This would certainly include the woman's family and home.

Therefore, as the husband and wife, during their own daily prayer, pray and study the Word of God separately then at an appointed time they pray together, the result is the power of agreement is activated. They are in position to take authority over obstacles and bear good fruit. They can receive instructions, guidance, wisdom, strategies and for some circumstances miracles from the Lord to help them smoothly manage and keep peace in their household. They will gain victory and accomplish the vision not only for their household but the vision given to the head of the house by the Lord which will ultimately affect their entire family.

The Lord has given the "male" man and the "female" man authority in the earth to take dominion over living creatures, the environment and their circumstances. Genesis 1:26 states God the Father made a decision that included God the Son and God the Holy Spirit to make mankind in their image and give them complete authority in the earth. Genesis 1:27 says, *"So God created man in His own image, in the image and likeness of God He created him; male and female He created them."*

Furthermore, in Genesis 1:28 it says, "And God blessed *them* and said to *them*, Be fruitful, multiply, and fill the earth, and subdue it [using all its vast resources in the service of God and man]; and have dominion..." Being created in His image would include His Spirit giving birth to their spirit as God breathed His Spirit into mankind and gave man the very life he has (John 4:24, Gen. 2:7 and I Thessalonians 5:23). His image would also reflect His character (the fruit of His Spirit, Gal. 5:22-23) and have reflections of God's glory which was their physical covering before they fell.

Also notice, God fully recognized the woman's presence from the very beginning when He addressed them both by blessing and speaking to them and giving them instructions even though the only one present in His sight was the "male" Adam (Adam means man, mankind or natural man in Hebrew). The "female" Adam at the time was a "hidden support" inside of the male as a *rib* or his side and did not appear until Gen. 2:21-22 when God brought her forth from the male Adam and built her up into a wo-man (man with a womb), Gen. 2:23. Notice the Lord did not have to breathe life into the woman He only built her up and brought her to the man because she (her spirit) was already alive inside of the "male."

So why was God addressing them both since the "male" man was the only one present? God made mankind in His image and likeness. God is a Spirit (a Spiritual Being according to John 4:24). So, the true person is a spiritual being that lives in a physical body that possesses a soul which is comprised of their mind, will and emotions. Mankind is part spirit, soul and body, I Thess. 5:23.

Therefore, the Lord was communicating with both of their *spirits* as He is a Spirit Himself and communicates with humans from His Spirit to our spirit. Remember also, a married couple has **supernaturally become one in the spirit** in God's sight upon saying their wedding vows, therefore, when He speaks to the husband or wife He is speaking to them concerning the plan He has for them both. (See *God's Way and Marriage, Chapter One* for further details on this subject.)

A Wife's Key Responsibilities May Not be Her Only Calling, Profession or Options

The capacities to nurture and be a helper are both key functions that keep a household lovable, disciplined, organized and functional. **However, these are not the only assignments or occupation a married woman has.** In the Traditional Nuclear Family, a married woman's primary, and in most cases *only* role, was to support her husband in his career and to help raise their children. And there is nothing wrong with that, it is expected if she is a wife and mother.

However, if a wife's value and identity are measured *only* with reference to her husband and children never in terms of *herself* as an individual with self-worth, goals, desires or dreams according to experts she can become and feel increasingly as a person without identity.

During the fifties and sixties era the media portrayed the Traditional Nuclear Family wife and mother as a person who was unsupported, isolated and considered somewhat unimportant by the world's standard and many times bored with the same routine. *We understand God desires that a wife's highest priority is her family and home but is that her only priority?* Except for the fulfillment she was a good wife and mother, **which is highly commended** especially for the strengthening of the family in any society, this is enough for some women **but is it enough for every woman?**

My answer would have to be no. Women are individuals with different callings on their lives like all other human beings on the planet. They are called to fulfill their God-given purpose as well.

In my personal life I've had the experience of working for years in different corporations doing various types of work which included litigation and the trust department in banking. I also have years of experience as a homemaker as well as overseeing a home-based business. In addition, I am an author and am now running a ministry corporation alongside my husband, which I feel is my true calling and purpose.

I can truly say from experience that each endeavor had its own season and I was anointed for each one of those seasons because it was done in God's timing and will for my life. If I missed God, He helped me catch up and got me back on track as I yielded to His leading.

Furthermore, I was anointed to operate in each season with a spirit of wisdom, excellence and provision because *I chose to wait on God.* Waiting on and moving in the Lord's timing will change you and renew your strength and power. His Word says, "But those who wait on the LORD Shall renew *their* strength; They shall mount up with wings like eagles, They shall run and not be weary, They shall walk and not faint" (give up), Isaiah 40:31 NKJV. Being faithful to trust Him will preserve you because "He preserves the faithful," Ps. 31:23.

This is the key to the Proverbs 31 woman, to move or flow with the Spirit of God in His timing and season with God's wisdom and instructions. It will preserve and enable you to accomplish what He purposed for your life in each given season. Is that to say we won't ever miss God? Of course not, but if we do, because we are striving to follow His leading, He will place us back on track and raise us up, launch us out and give us the victory.

The key is to do things God's Way. It will require faith and the renewing of your mind which will be a process, Romans 12:2. If you remain faithful and learn how to align your thinking with

Almighty God, you will reap the fruit (benefits) of it.

A woman should also have options. God Himself, did not say being a homemaker, similar to the early sitcoms was a woman's *only* calling, occupation or purpose for being on this earth. *Remember, there is a season for everything, she needs to know what season she is in and yield to the leading of the Holy Spirit.*

A woman should not yield to restrictions of people when God is clearly speaking and opening doors. Doors of opportunities to utilize the gifts, skills, talents or education that He has imparted in or provided for her, for His purpose and glory.

A woman or wife like anyone else needs to be willing, obedient, available and all she can be to fulfill her purpose and assignment from the Lord. God uses women in many capacities, in addition to the role of a homemaker or other than the role of one. So, who has the right to limit her capacity? Proverbs 31:13-19, 26, 31. The Bible also says, "We must obey God rather than men" Acts 5:29.

If a married woman is sensing God would have her to step out and expand in more areas, then **(1)** *she and her husband should seek God, pray and discuss it* so God's perfect will for their family, in that season will be done. Also, she is to be mindful that this should not be done at the neglect of her present responsibilities as a wife and mother. Therefore, to save time and strength **(2)** *she should ask for divine wisdom and proceed to plan well,* as well as seek God early for instructions and **(3)** *to* *delegate work* and not try to do everything herself so she can plant fruitful vines in her vineyard (so her work will be productive and multiply in a good way and she can still enjoy her life and family), Prov. 31:15-18 Amplified Bible.

Individuals as well as families should be in their "set place" spiritually and physically. For instance, where they fellowship (attend church and/or bible study), live and work needs to be in God's will and timing for that season so His grace will abound with favor. This will ensure that when God is doing different things in their lives they can operate with full authority and receive the breakthroughs and victories that come with it.

Will this stop all storms from happening in her family's life? No. *God did not say we would not have trials and tribulations,* when the *storms come* we are to *resist them* and know *He will be in them with us* to guide us through. At the same time, we will become stronger and will have learned a great deal as well as received a fresh anointing along with breakthroughs and promises being fulfilled.

John 16:33 Addresses the Issue of Trials and Tribulations,

> I have told you these things, so that in Me you may have [perfect] peace *and* confidence. In the world you have tribulation *and* trials *and* distress *and* frustration; but be of good cheer [take courage; be confident, certain,

undaunted]! For I have overcome the world. [I have deprived it of power to harm you and have conquered it for you.]

But on the other hand, *if a wife is not going forth toward her purpose because people's opinions have superseded what God has said,* then her resistance to God will give place to the adversary and the "divine purpose" for her life will be in jeopardy.

For example, she could open a door for delays, hindrances, spiritual attacks on her marriage and home, physical attacks on her health, business and in other areas, simply because through her disobedience she has moved out of the perfect will of God for her life. In other words, she is no longer under God's full protection because of her choices.

A husband who is hindering his wife from answering any call from God or for fulfilling any assignment God has given her, needs to understand even though he is the head of his home, *Jesus (Yeshua) is the High Priest and final authority of every Believer's home.* Therefore, his wife as a Believer, must obey the final authority; the One Who knows what is best and only does what is for our good. If not, it could affect everyone in the household to some degree.

God anoints people who are willing and obedient to fulfill His plan. He is not limited to use only adults, or only males, or only females, or even only children. He is not limited to singles or the married. Neither is He limited to gender, age or color but *you can limit God in your life with disobedience to His perfect will and timing.* His only criterion is do hey have a willing and obedient heart.

This is not intended to add any type of pressure or stress of trying to find God's perfect will and timing for your life. God is loving, patient and all knowing. He will gently guide you by His Spirit as you spend time with Him in prayer and in His Word. You will become sensitive to His leading as He gives you instructions and directions to follow. This will lead you into and keep you in His perfect will and timing for your life.

The Traditional Nuclear Family teaches the wife she is to do all the adapting to her husband in order for their marriage to be successful. ***Biblical principles tell us that both partners need to make an effort to adapt and get to know one another.*** In Ephesians 5:21 it says "Be subject to one another out of reverence for Christ." Being subject or submitting basically is honoring and respecting one another in the fear of God. *Therefore, the both of them need to know and understand each other's needs, wants and desires to fulfill this mandate.*

Biblical Illustrations of Different Kinds of Options Women Have Including Those According to Proverbs Chapter 31

In various books of the Bible there are recordings of women who were married or single; plain or beautiful and how God used many of them mightily such as: **The Jewish Queen Esther** (Hadassah was her Hebrew name) who was married to the Persian King, Ahasuerus was used by God to save the nation of Jewish people by risking her own life Esther 4:16; and how He used the **Prophet Deborah**, a patriotic military advisor who went to war, was a judge of Israel and a married woman, Judges 4:4-10.

God also had **Prophet Miriam** lead a nation of women in praise to God after crossing the Red Sea, Exod. 15:20, 21; **Hannah,** was the ideal mother, I Sam. 1:20; 2:19; **The Queen of Sheba,** also referred to as the Queen of Ethiopia who was a direct descendant of Ham and of Shem. She was extremely wealthy and responsible for a kingdom. She also gave birth to King Solomon's son Menelek I Kings 10:1; 2 Chron. 9:1, 9, 12. And let's not forget **Mary Magdalene, Joanna and Mary the mother of James and other women with them** who reported (ministered) the Good News (The Gospel) of Jesus Christ for the first time in history by anyone. They were chosen to report the news Jesus had risen from the grave to the apostles and others Luke 24: 3-10, 22; Matt. 28:7, 10; John 20:11-18.

The Lord has not changed His mind. He still uses women mightily to minister, teach, preach and publish the Word. The Word of God says in Psalm 68:11, "The Lord gives the word [of power]; the women who bear *and* publish [the news] are a great host."

There was also a family of women who were honored by God and inherited land when they requested it. Their father who had died in the wilderness on the way to the Promise Land had no sons and his daughters did not want their father's name to be removed from his family by not inheriting his portion of the Promise Land.

So, Moses brought it before God and the Lord said "the daughters of Zelophehad are justified and speak correctly. You shall surely give them an inheritance among their father's brethren..." Numbers 27: 4-8. This law was then given by God to all that a woman can inherit her father's land if she has no brothers (v. 8).

Job 42:15 Demonstrates His Daughters Also Received an Inheritance,

> Nowhere in all the land were there found women as beautiful as Job's daughters, and their father granted them an inheritance along with their brothers.

In this passage, Job is a type and shadow of Father God Who desires to bless all of His children with an inheritance. Male or female God is no respecter of persons, Acts 10:34.

Unfortunately, certain countries and people chose not to listen to and obey this instruction and women were prevented from owning property and businesses even if they could afford to purchase. A plan constructed by Satan to keep women at the mercy of men for their livelihood as well as far from their destiny.

Thus, another reason many women rebelled was because again oppression and limitations were set by Satan through man and not by God.

And lastly, are the **two women** found in the book of Luke 10:40-42 one who chose housework and complained and the other who chose according to Jesus *"the one thing that was needful*, the good part, which shall not be taken away." The good part being referred to by Jesus that she could learn directly from Him the ways of God, learn who she was in Christ, and what her assignment or purpose in this earth would be. She could become the *Proverbs 31 woman* that was so highly spoken of in terms of being an excellent wife, mother, woman of God as well as a successful businesswoman.

The Wife of Noble Character, Proverbs 31:10-31 NIV [1]

Women may play many roles in a successful family relationship. This appears to be a composite picture of the ideal wife and mother. One woman could hardly perform all the functions mentioned within one day. The woman is equally active in home and business duties. She is trusted by her husband and seeks to help him at all times. She works hard, makes difficult decisions, earns and invests money well, is compassionate and helpful to the needy, is prepared for the future, and has wisdom to teach other people. She has earned a high reputation in her family, in the business world, and in the community. *All of this is possible because her life is centered on God. The Bible thus challenges women to use their talents in as many areas as possible to bring honor to God, their family, and themselves.*

Many women as well as men are not aware of the Biblical order of submission. Therefore, assume in "blind submission" a woman is to be obedient to any male, which is not biblically true. *The Biblical order of submission is on a broader scale which would bring a greater harvest for obedience.*
Women are to submit (honor and respect) delegated authority beginning with submitting to God first; to delegated leaders in Godly appointed authoritative positions; to her government and to her own husband, not to just any man. Submission to God-appointed leadership will always cause God's favor to flow in one's life.

This submission is measured by one's love for God. Love for God gives a woman the grace (the power, the enablement) to submit to the delegated authority in her life. When she does, it is because she realizes she is cooperating with the will of Father God whose authority supersedes any delegated authority in her life. Simply because God has all authority in heaven and earth, Mt. 28:18.

In doing for others she is not to be submitted to any type of abuse. Often submission implies a superior/inferior, master/slave, head/foot type of relationship when God never ordained this as part of a woman's role.

The Lord's submission (because she is doing all unto God) will enable her to be a person who is strong and secure enough with who she is so she can humble herself in such a way to be submissive to God's will first.

Just like the Lord gives the right woman the ability, wisdom and creativity to help her husband, God also gives the right man the wisdom and ability to be the head of his family. Therefore, a wife can help her husband by doing things to assist and not take over but help him to be the man of the house God called him to be.

For example, just one of the things a wife can do to honor and show respect to her husband is when you are both *in public* and someone *asks him a question*, let him answer the question. Give him a little time, men process information differently than women and he may need a minute to find out how he feels about something or how he prefers to word his answer. Most women can be impatient with this because they do not require time to process anything, they hear and they speak, it is as simple as that.

However, spiritually mature women have learned to wait and allow their husbands to answer the question. A simple act like this will esteem him, build him up and give him respect in front of others. Sometimes it's alright to take the lead when others are speaking to him but not all the time as some of us will do. Small things like this will keep things in balance and help things continue to flow smoothly in your household.

If you find you are making nearly all of the decisions that is out of order and it is just a matter of time with reoccurrences like this and others before something collapses. Try building his confidence up and his leadership skills will improve as you step back and allow him to lead.

Some women are probably thinking, well if I step back we will all be in the poor house. Not necessarily, unless you are dealing with someone who is doing destructive things that would destroy the home. I am basically talking about things that are within normal circumstances occurring in the home.

The Proverbs 31 Woman Sheds Even More Light on the Role of a Wife

The following passage in Proverbs 31:10-31 (paraphrased) describes the woman as a wife, a mother and a successful business woman:

She is praised by her husband (v28);

She is loved and called blessed by her children (v28);

She is a homemaker and successful business woman (vs 14, 16 and 24);

She feeds her family spiritual and natural food as she teaches them the revelation of God's Word (vs14-15).

She and her family wear the finest clothing (v13 and vs 21-22);

Her husband is well known in the city and respected in the community (v23);

She keeps up her physical appearance as she is spiritually, mentally and physically fit (v17);

She is a woman that reverently fears the Lord and reaches out her filled-hands to the needy (vs15, 20);

Her husband trusts and relies and believes in her securely (v11);

She is a woman who in her kindness speaks godly Wisdom as she gives counsel and instruction (v26);

She is a person that delegates authority as well as a woman who was not afraid to work (vs15, 19);

She is a woman who is far more precious than jewels and her value is far above rubies or pearls (v10).

A Proverbs 31 Woman - Amplified Bible Footnote:

"Many daughters have done...nobly and well...but you excel them all." What a glowing description here recorded of this woman in private life, this "capable, intelligent, and virtuous woman" of Prov. 31! It means she has done more than Miriam, the one who led a nation's women in praise to God (Exod. 15:20, 21); Deborah, the patriotic military advisor (Judg. 4:4-10); Ruth, the woman of constancy (Ruth 1:16); Hannah, the ideal mother (I Sam. 1:20; 2:19); the Shunammite, the hospitable woman (II Kings 4:8-10); Huldah, the woman who revealed God's secret message to national leaders (II Kings 22:14); and even more than Queen Esther, the woman who risked sacrificing her life for her people (Esth. 4:16). **In what way did she "excel them all"? In Her spiritual and practical devotion to God, which permeated every area and relationship of her life.** All seven of the Christian virtues (II Peter 1:5) are there, like colored threads in a tapestry. Her secret, which is open to everyone, is the Holy Spirit's climax to the story, and to this book. In Prov. 31:30, it becomes clear that the "reverent and worshipful fear of the Lord," which is "the beginning (the chief and choice part) of **Wisdom**" (Prov. 9:10), **is put forth as the true foundation for a life which is valued by God and her husband** as "far above rubies *or* pearls" (Prov. 31:10). (Emphasis added.)

Chapter 7

Other Family Roles: Child, Adolescent, Adult Child and Extended Family

For all those who are Born-again Believers, your first ministry is your family because that is the order of God. Therefore, this comes before our concerns with our place of employment and our businesses.

Why is this the order? Because if the vision God gave you superseded loving and being kind to one another it would come against His own Word. **First** of all, He said that we should love one another, John 13:34 and I John 4:12. **Second,** if we relied solely on our own works to supply a need we would not need to trust God and we would leave Him out of the equation.

We should trust Him and as we are obedient to His Word our need is met with abundance for our business, ministry or income from work. And any other way the Lord chooses to bless because of our obedience, one's ability to follow instructions. We in turn can be a blessing to our family, extended family including the elderly in our family, friends and widows and orphans in the Kingdom of God.

Biblical Instructions for the Role of a Child

The role of a child may vary with their age. Their functions in the household may change as given by their delegated authority, their parents.

A child should have a prayer closet -- a time set aside to worship and talk to God and build their personal relationship with Him. They should also have time set aside to read the Word of God. This could be after their prayer time or scheduled in before or after homework. The age to start their personal prayer time can be as young as five, six or seven it depends on the child.

My natural daughter was already Born-again, Spirit-filled and praying in her spiritual prayer language at the age of three and at that time I was surprised because I was not aware children that young could be filled with the Infilling of the Holy Spirit. However, to be consistent with a regular prayer time I would think a little older would be better. It should be encouraged according to their attention span and understanding.

She prayed as she was led by the Spirit of God at home, in church or when we were with other Spirit-filled people. At preschool she laid hands on sick students and they were healed. Their parents inquired and their child told them our daughter prayed for them. (Child-like faith through a child works too!)

When my natural son was only nine years old he was up each morning at six a.m. to pray for thirty minutes. At this time, he started hearing the Lord speak to him. I later encouraged him to write down what he heard. He would record what he heard on a pad of paper next to the chair he sat on to pray. Afterwards he would share with me what he had heard.

I knew he was truly hearing from God because I heard many of the same prophetic words earlier on the very same morning when I was in my prayer time. God was confirming what He told me through my son and at the same time He was teaching both of us how to hear His voice and learn His ways and will for our lives.

After we became a Blended Family one of the guidelines in our home was that each person had their own daily prayer time in the morning. This applied only to the children still living at home, two were already grown. During this time my husband's natural son began having a number of prophetic dreams of which many had already come to pass. Television was not permitted during the early morning hours because that was their time as individuals to spend with God. My husband and I rose up much earlier than the children so we could spend more time in God's presence.

As a result, they all have a relationship with the Lord, and they are Born-again Spirit-filled Christians. They can discern the voice of God or how He communicates with each one of them on a one-on-one basis. Each one has seen God move mightily on their behalf. They know He is real!

In addition, they know personally that hell is real and some have even heard Satan's voice try to frighten or deceive them. Our youngest has seen angels as well as demonic spirits. Our children are aware there is more to this life than what we see with our natural eyes. There is much activity in the invisible realm even more so than what we see in the natural.

Some parents make the mistake of not leading the way and directing them toward the will and Word of God that would empower them. His truth found in the Word will give them a strong foundation in life because of the relationship they developed with Him while growing up.

Ephesians 6:4 tells Parents how to Raise their Children,

Rear them [tenderly] in the training and discipline and the counsel and admonition of the Lord.

God told all parents to do this, train them up the way they should go, meaning train them up the right way, in the Word of God because that is the standard they should live by. Notice I did not say train them up in "religion" basically having a form of godliness coupled with a lot of rules and regulation most of which have nothing to do with the Lord.

But instead show them how to *have a personal relationship so they can know God for themselves* and have the privilege of fellowshipping and learning directly from Him. That is what will make the difference in their lives.

The Lord will Teach Your Children Directly, Isaiah 54:13,

> And all your [spiritual] children shall be disciples [taught by the Lord and obedient to His will], and great shall be the peace and undisturbed composure of your children.

Some parents feel they should let their child find their own way and faith after they are older, either teens or young adults. Even though, these same parents will enforce school work, after school activities, sports, music, dance and so on but *not enforce and oversee or even introduce the most important part of their upbringing.* This may have happened because they probably had a bad experience with "church people" themselves, or because they have been told "religion" is a personal thing people need to discover for themselves.

Or evolution was taught in their schools; or perhaps their parents do not have a personal relationship with God and did not know the value of knowing Him. Then there are those that do not know God and do not desire to believe there is one and prefer to be an atheist or agnostic.

Many parents have left their children to learn the hard way, they will need a Savior in this life. In the meantime, for all those that do not know they will learn by experience there is good and evil in this world. Unfortunately, they will probably be told they should just flow with whatever happens in life because there is nothing they or anyone can do about it.

Parents, the Holy Spirit in your child when they are a Born-again Believer is the same Holy Spirit inside of you if they are a Born-again Believer. A spirit has no age and never dies. Only our body ages and passes away. Your body is a house or home for your spirit (who is the real person, the real you) and a home for your soul (your mind, will and emotions).

Therefore, it is not cruel to help your child develop a relationship with God by taking them to a good Word-based Spirit-filled church. A church where the fivefold ministry is in operation (Eph. 4:11-12); bible study and telling them to pray and read the Bible on their own, 2 Tim. 2:15.

If you are a Believer in Jesus then you should know you have a Helper inside of you. This Helper's name is Holy Spirit, the Third Person of the Godhead. In John 14:26 it says He is our, "Comforter (Counselor, Helper, Intercessor, Advocate, Strengthener, Standby), the Holy Spirit, Whom the Father will send in My name [in My place, to represent Me and act on My behalf], He will teach you all things. And He will cause you to recall (will remind you of, bring to your remembrance) everything I have told you."

Holy Spirit was sent as a Promise from Father God (YHVH) as a free gift from Heaven to be with us and in us, Acts 1:4. He came once Jesus ascended into heaven Acts 1:9-11. When we and our children receive salvation, this same Holy Spirit comes to dwell inside of us. Therefore, instead of putting your trust in your own efforts, many different rules, regulations and methods why not simply lean on God trusting Him and, in His grace, help you raise your children? Not doing things in your own strength but truly by the wisdom, strength and grace of Almighty God.

When there is a situation with your children you can always go to Father God in the name of Jesus and the power of Holy Spirit will respond. As you rely on Holy Spirit and not solely on your own mind in raising your children you can ask and receive, Matthew 7:7. He will assist you in different ways with answers, guidance, and whatever is needed because He knows the heart and the root of all problems.

For example, there may be something troubling your child to the point they are very disturbed. It won't help to question them, guess the problem, feel sorry for them or even try to use discipline to get them to open up. These tactics may only frustrate you and them even more. Keep in mind Holy Spirit already has the answer. As we seek Him first He will open and soften hearts and give you the words that will truly bless your child and show them they can trust you and trust the God you worship and serve.

The Holy Spirit can directly reveal to you what is wrong. Or He may have you ask certain questions that will show your child they can speak to you and they share their heart. Many times, the child is having a battle in their mind. As they speak you can recognize the lie from the adversary they are listening to that is causing them torment. You can expose the lie, correct it with truth and encourage them. More than likely it was something to attack their self-esteem, confidence and identity.

As you and your household stay submitted to the Spirit of God He will lead you in different ways to solve issues that arise. He may have you read a scripture, share a story, sometimes give a consequence or a hug and kiss to reassure them of your love for them. Maybe the Holy Spirit will have the two of you talk more about the circumstance or maybe just be still and pray while He works it out.

The entire household should be encouraged to seek God first. It will always be better if we choose to live by faith calling on God and being led by Holy Spirit rather than our own strength or some self-help book.

The day may come, if you did not teach them, you will wish you had. *You would have been able to rest in the fact they have a foundation to fall back on and to remember what is truly important in life, Luke 15.* Being exposed to Truth will give them something to compare to when they hear a lie or a lot of nonsense from people who do not know the Word and the ways of God. Your child may sound foolish to them because they are hearing something they cannot comprehend, I Corinthians 2:14.

As a result, they will try to push their unbelief onto your child but if your child is grounded with wisdom and understanding of the Word they should not be moved by other's false doctrines and opinions Eph. 4:14.

The Word of God gives specific instructions in the bringing up of our children that will give them a strong foundation for the rest of their lives. One of those scriptures is as follows:

Proverbs 22:6 tells us,

> Train up a child in the way he should go [and in keeping with his individual gift or bent], and when he is old he will not depart from it.

This is speaking directly to bringing them up the right way, having the righteousness of God (His way of doing and being right -- Matthew 6:33). The Word will be the foundation for them to rest upon and make decisions for the rest of their lives when they are taught the principles in the Bible.

Two other versions of Proverbs 22:6 were equally nice: The Passion Translation (TPT) says, *"Dedicate your children to God and point them in the way that they should go, and the values they've learned from you will be with them for life."* And another is in The Message Bible (MSG) says, "Point your kids in the right direction-- when they're old they won't be lost."

God commanded the parents to do this, it is not the government's responsibility, nor the schools to teach our children who God is and His ways of doing things, it is our responsibility.

Children are sensitive, trusting and believing in their hearts and are usually not hardened towards the things of God, so it would be easier to teach them while they are young. During this time, it would also be good for them to talk to God about their purpose in this life. To ask Him in prayer what His purpose for their life is?

So many children grow up and still not have a clue as to why they are on the face of this earth. Suicide among teens is enough evidence of that. Young people with *a vision and dream for their future, hope and a personal relationship with God* (I did not say religion or having been forced to church every week) rarely kill themselves. They already know there is more to life than what they have experienced and life could be exciting if they have truly given it to God.

People are always asking children and teens, "So what do you want to be when you grow up?" *When the question should be, what has God said that He has planned for your life, Jeremiah 29:11? Has He revealed your purpose in life to you yet?* When they are young and have heard from the Lord as to what He has planned for their lives this would eliminate a lot of confusion later.

Pressure will also stop some parents from interfering and trying to dictate what they want their children to be when they grow up. It would also give everyone a peace of mind if they are Believers and understand how to live by faith. If it is God's plan for a child to take over the family business then God will let them know and anoint them to operate it in an excellent way.

There is such a thing as a generational calling or anointing God purposed for the offspring to carry on. God does raise up families to do certain deeds in His Kingdom (His Kingdom includes marketplace businesses and work outside of the church building).

As the young person seeks God, He will reveal to him or her what He has in store for his or her life and confirm it in their heart. He could also confirm it through strangers, prophets or other Believers. In addition, it can be confirmed through apparent gifts, talents or interests in certain areas the child already possesses or anyway God chooses to confirm what He has said.

Although remember that a person's gift is not always their purpose. Sometimes the gift is there to help with the purpose. Whatever His plan is it will always be better than any plan he or she or the parents could come up with.

God's plan fills the voids, completes and causes one to be content and secure in what they are doing once they make a decision to allow God to enable them to do it. He will also anoint, equip, train, and make all the provisions and give the abundance for His purpose in your child's life.

They would only need to rest in Him and follow the leading of His Spirit to make the right connections, be in the right place at the right time and/or attend the right schools for them if that is required.

Believe it or not, not everyone is supposed to "go away to college" that is not the plan for everyone. That is worldly Greek-minded thinking that keeps everyone in a box using the same formula to arrive at the same designation and as we can see many settle into dead-end jobs or boring careers that rob them of precious time with their families, if they even take time to start one.

Why does this happen? Because many people never bother to ask God what His plan is and as a result they are operating and functioning in jobs or careers or businesses they were not anointed, designed or equipped to do and even though they can handle the work they are not fulfilled and are miserable.

In addition, they are encouraged to get multiple degrees to be able to compete in the market place and so forth. The stress, money and fear of failure all play a part because they are relying solely on what "they can accomplish" according to what man not God says success is. Not to mention higher education is big business that uses millions of dollars in advertising to pressure people to go in this direction.

Having a higher education is good. If that is something you have in your heart then it is for you. But let's not make it mandatory for every human being to have in order to be successful. Many times, a trade you love or a small business to help others or running a corporation is best fitted for your child when they become of age. Whatever it is once the young person finds what they were purposed for the contentment, interest and anointing will be there to help them reach their goals. *As long as you are in the will of God and doing what He purposed for your life you are a success*!

A Part of the Biblical Role of a Child is to Obey, Honor and Respect their Parents

Ephesians 6:1-3 tells us,

> Children, obey your parents in the Lord [as His representatives], for this is just and right. Honor (esteem and value as precious) your father and your mother – this is the first commandment with a promise. That all may be well with you and that you may live long on the earth. (Also see, Exodus 20:12.)

We are in the *End-Times, a new season has begun* and the prophets have foretold the condition and mindset of those who are not Believers. How they including children will treat their parents and others.

2 Timothy 3:2-4 Foretells of Unbelievers During the End-Times or Last Days,

> For people will be lovers of self *and* [utterly] self-centered, lovers of money *and* aroused by an inordinate [greedy] desire for wealth, proud *and* arrogant *and*

contemptuous boasters. They will be abusive (blasphemous, scoffing), disobedient to parents, ungrateful, unholy *and* profane).

[They will be] without natural [human] affection (callous and inhuman), relentless (admitting of no truce or appeasement); [they will be] slanderers (false accusers, troublemakers), intemperate *and* loose in morals *and* conduct, uncontrolled *and* fierce, haters of good.

[They will be] treacherous [betrayers], rash, [and] inflated with self-conceit. [They will be] lovers of sensual pleasures *and* vain amusements more than *and rather* than lovers of God.

When and if we listen to God, Who knows the beginning from the end; Who knows all things and has the power to change things; Who has sent His prophets of whom many were used to record in the Bible warnings for us to take heed to (pay attention to) that would help guide us in life.

If we listen to God we can help our children while they are young. If we choose to follow simple instructions that are preventive measures for preserving the family. Then we as Believers should not behave in the way of the world, if trained by

Holy Spirit, Second Timothy three's description does not have to apply to your household.

Studies show children who have a personal relationship with God at the time of their parents' divorce are quicker to recover in a healthier way than those who did not. Many times, those who did not have a relationship with their heavenly Father, their Savior or the Comforter would turn to friends, sex, gangs, drugs, alcohol and rebellion to pay back those who hurt them I Cor. 15:33. Many begin by seeking relief but are tempted to go in the wrong direction. They end up hurting themselves because of the lifestyle they are living.

These things only compounded their problems and as a result they stayed in bondage longer. Whereas the child who has some history with God and knows of His ways and His will, will clearly have the advantage if they turn to Him and do what He says. *When they trust Him to make it better, heal their broken heart and they choose to forgive, pray for their parents and not turn against all authority they will discover a peace and freedom.*

Children will have an option to do all in the natural or flow with the spiritual and receive supernatural healing and intervention. They will have a peace and be able to continue to hear God speak and give them direction. They can also in turn use what they have learned to help someone else who may be experiencing the same thing.

Suggestions to Help Children Make Adjustments

- Learn to really listen to your children and make eye contact as often as possible. Be a good role model in your home for your family.

- Help them to feel better about themselves and show them what the Word of God has to say about them (either you do it or find a good Bible study to attend).

- Showing them you have confidence and believe in them and they are pleasing to God will certainly help them feel more surer about themselves.

- The Word of God will help them develop a strong moral value system, knowing right from wrong where they can make decisions based on truth, facts and God's revelation.

- Your family should be aware of your attitudes and habits regarding drugs, alcohol and pre-marital sex. Share information about these subjects with them and never rely on the schools, their friends or even church meetings to discuss these issues with your children especially without your input.

- Advise them on how to resist peer pressure. Teach them they cannot please everyone and should not try. They are only obligated to please a loving God with their faith and be themselves. Teach them to say "no," not everyone will like it or like them but they must do what is best for their well-being.

- Encourage and teach them the proper foods to eat. What people eat does affect their behavior especially if there is too much sugar or fast foods in their diet.

- You as a parent need to plan the meals and lunches and have them participate so they can learn how to select and prepare the better foods for their bodies and future families.

- Talk with other parents who may have children your child's age or a Christian counselor or read Christian materials to keep up with current tips that work in today's society that will help your child grow and mature with godly character and without a lot of drama.

- Teach them not to be self-centered but to care about others. Also teach them to give of their time, and money to help others.

- It is wise to know certain signs that go with certain behaviors. For instance, if your child is involved with drugs or the wrong influences you should know the signs. Notice if there is a sudden change in their behavior in dressing, speech, moods, attitude, withdrawing from authority or being disrespectful to adults. Notice if there has been a change in their sleep patterns and their interests. Be aware and know your child. If you are too busy to do at least half of these suggestions then you are too busy and may need to adjust your schedule and rely more on God and less on yourself.

Many parents are working multiple jobs to make ends meet. This will truly be at the expense of their family. Only work *one* nine to five job and trust God for the rest. Tell God, I am doing this Your way and I expect You to help me. He said in His Word we are to come boldly before His throne. That does not mean with anger or disrespect but come expecting Him to hear you, fellowship and answer.

Hebrews 4:16 says,

> *Let us then fearlessly and confidently and boldly draw near to the throne* of grace (the throne of God's unmerited favor to us sinners), that we may receive mercy [for our failures] and find grace to help in good time for every good [appropriate help and well-timed help, coming just when we need it]. (Emphasis added.)

James 7:7-8 KJV says,

Ask, and it shall be given you, *seek,* and ye shall find; *knock,* and it shall be opened unto you: For everyone that asketh receiveth; and he that seeketh findeth; and to him that knocketh it shall be opened. (Emphasis added.)

Yes, He knows what you are in need of before you even ask, but He said to ask (pray), seek (study the Bible) and knock (praise and thanksgiving). Because of your free will and His divine order if you do this His way, you will see the results you desired in your heart.

Because of your effort your family will discover you genuinely care, are interested and you are willing to give of yourself with your time, energy and money to have a relationship with them. As you open yourself up and are transparent in order to be as honest as you can they will realize you are not perfect and they don't have to be perfect either.

Be a person who will put forth the effort to have a better and more joyful life with everyone in their household. *When your heart is sincere, they will feel loved and their needs will be met.* Any needs not met, hopefully, they will know the *One* who will supply all their needs and ask Him, for themselves. It is never too late to come to Him, just as you are.

Adolescents Require Affection and Attention

Parents and guardians please remember adolescents (the process or period of growth between childhood and young adult also known as the teenage years), are *not* mature adults. Independence is a part of the growth process and it should be given with supervision realizing of course each child is an individual with different personalities and characteristics and requires a different set of limitations.

Those limitations may be: bedtimes (which are just as important for teens who are still growing and need their rest as much as smaller children), eating dinner with the family as opposed to constantly eating junk food or even eating alone in their room in front of a television or computer most of the time and never having time for family outings, fellowship or other events.

Their social life also needs to be monitored by the parents to know who their teen is actually in contact with and who is an influence in their lives. Some teens may become upset if you seem to be too involved in their "personal life" but never distance yourself too far because that too is not really what they want or need.

They still need your love, approval and acceptance as they become a little distant in trying to find their way independent of you as they grow and learn more about themselves and other things in the world.

Some households do not experience the rebellion, the pulling away because the kids like their home and love their family and enjoy spending time with them. The communication is open and they like doing things together. This depends strictly on the family and the type of upbringing the child was exposed to (sense of security, humility, openness, godly ways, good communication, balance, roles defined and so forth).

Wise parents will listen and continue to give them attention. Stay active in their lives in certain areas whether they want it or not exercising wisdom and balance. Realize they are individuals and wise boundaries and limitations need to be set as mentioned above. In continuing to give them attention show them love with hugs and kisses on the cheek, even a kiss good night is welcomed at most ages. *People are never too old for proper affection in expressing love.* A little hug here and there or an encouraging pat on their shoulder can be so encouraging and bring healing.

However, each situation will warrant different behavior that is relevant to the type of family you are in. If it is a Blended, Foster or an Adopted Family you may not be dealing with your natural children and unless you know the history of a child, be cautious of how you approach and touch them. Many children in this society and others around the world are experiencing all types of abuse and have been exposed to things beyond their years. Many will need healing before they will allow anyone too close.

So, if you are rejected be aware and try to not take everything personally. Realize people are doing what is necessary for their survival not necessarily doing something on purpose to hurt someone else. Many times, those who are hurting will usually end up hurting others to some degree.

My kids looked forward to a kiss good night and felt special, loved and for some it offered a sense of security because each child is different with different needs. Many times, my husband and I would go into their room together and kiss them good night. This was at a time when most of them were already adolescents and some of them even stayed up longer than we did.

We have found many parents stopped expressing and showing love to their teens in this manner once they became a certain age and frankly that is sad because this is when the need for acceptance is the greatest. Teens generally will not ask for affection or attention like smaller children instead they act out their need by rebelling or in other ways to receive attention that may be embarrassing or hurtful to their parents or themselves.

If they cannot get the attention, affirmation, love and approval from you they need they will find someone who will give them the emotional support they desire. Furthermore, it will probably be from the wrong person or source with the wrong advice and motive. They will attempt to feed input into your child's life which could be very damaging and cause you and your family great distress for months or even years.

To avoid such problems from the beginning do not give up your role or authority as the parent in your child's life no matter what the age (small child, pre-teen or teenager and in some cases young adults who still live at home). Parents should accept their role as parents and their adult responsibilities so their children can remain in their role as children, growing and maturing at a healthy pace for them. They should not be forced too soon into adult roles.

Parents should offer comfort and security to their children instead of, as many do, look to their children to comfort and console them and allow or force adult responsibilities and/or circumstances on their children.

I believe teens should help in the home especially with keeping their room and bathroom clean. Also, pick-up after themselves, organize their wardrobe and put their clothes away. Maintaining the laundry for the younger children is an adult responsibility. When the older children make snacks or meals they should clean up the portion of the kitchen they utilized.

They can also have other responsibilities in the household but those that will not drastically interfere with their education, quality family time, play time and their social time nor their time to go to sleep and rest. If possible, a housekeeper is always nice to help lighten the load and a part-time chef wouldn't hurt either. But if these don't quite fit into your spending plan (budget) the family can all work together to lighten the load if both parents or a single-parent works outside of the home.

Parents who assign adolescents the responsibility to take charge, maintain and run the entire household with the planning of meals, and most or all of the cooking, cleaning, shopping, taking care of the younger children, handling the mail and bills, even having a part time job to add to the family income, please note these are the responsibilities of the parent(s) or an adult in the household.

To train a child is one thing but to hand over all or most of your adult responsibilities because you are *too busy* is no excuse and, in the end, you will have serious consequences including robbing them of precious memories of their childhood. A good healthy balance should apply in every area of your life and theirs.

You are responsible to create a loving secure atmosphere and environment in and around your home where your child feels you are in charge, in control of your life and doing your part. You as the parent should know or learn how to adjust your personal schedules and set your priorities following first of all God's instructions and order in which to do things. Ask for wisdom daily as to what He would have you to do in addition to the agenda you have scheduled for yourself and place His request first.

Read time management or business information to find out how to set proper priorities and do proper scheduling of your time. It could be you are involved in too many outside activities, you are running too many unnecessary errands for yourself, your extended family or friends or others. Maybe you are involved in too much community activity. It could be you are simply working on a job too many hours; working overtime or week-ends or having a second or third job especially if you are a single parent.

Be aware this is a trap to wear you out and rob you of years of time that could be spent enjoying your family, friends and yourself. And you would say, "But we have to eat, the bills must be paid!" And I would say, "I agree, but there is a better way!"

God can make provision for part-time help to come in or move on the hearts of people to help you. They could be a part of your Spiritual Family or a member of your Extended Family or a good friend who will help lighten the load. He can give you such revelation and lead your footsteps on a path where you have every favor and provision met. We must learn how to receive. It is as important as knowing how to give of your time, your talents and so forth.

The Lord said, He "will liberally supply your every need according to His riches in glory by Christ Jesus" Philippians 4:19. He is your Helper, Hebrews 13:6 and John 16:7. God also said He "...came that they may have *and* enjoy life, and have it in abundance (to the full, till it overflows)" John 10:10. He will make a way for you out of no way and all He asks, is you *ask, believe, receive* and *trust Him* to follow through.

If we follow *God's order* He will honor and help us. When we set our priorities with His order in mind He will give us divine information, revelation and supernatural help to assist us with our family and lifestyle. Do the things that are in your heart to do for your family. Spending time to have conversation or take a walk and walk the dog with your kids.

Doing simple inexpensive things, where you can give your undivided attention will be greatly appreciated by your children and pleasing to God. *Showing acts of love and kindness are attributes of God and when you walk in love, you're walking with God, for God is Love,* I John 4:16. Remember, He is as close to you as you will let Him be at any given time.

James 4:8 says,

> Draw nigh (close) to God, and He will draw nigh (close) to you...

Set your schedule so you will have time once or twice a month or more to spend with each child on a one on one basis. Offer advice and suggestions that will enable that child or teen to overcome certain obstacles in their lives. For example, James may need advice for a workable schedule and study habits to enable him to complete high school or prepare for college and to give praises and encouragement during this difficult time.

Janet on the other hand has mastered those things and has a great relationship with God and is following His plan for her life. However, she may need advice or training on her organizational skills, or money management and how to balance a checkbook or how to handle herself in mixed company. Some of these things seem routine to an adult yet they can be extremely stressful to a young person coupled with all the other demands in society today.

Both will need godly and moral training, discipline for proper sleeping and eating habits and so forth. *Your child may be a born leader, but a person who is untrained and unloved as a child will more than likely grow up to be a wild,* undisciplined and rebellious adult if they are not given an opportunity to develop godly character.

You may think, "It is too late they are older and rebellious, I'm tired and stressed, and don't know what to do. I do not know God, I do not know the Word of God (the Bible) and I cannot teach them something I do not know. On top of all that, my teen is not talking about their personal life or needs with me; they are hiding things, lying about their whereabouts and who their friends are and what they are doing."

Parent(s) relax, take a deep breath and humble yourself knowing you cannot do this alone. *Say a simple but sincere prayer from your heart and invite Jesus into your life and ask Him to help you.* A simple prayer and a sincere heart will get through to the throne room any day. God and His mercy will reveal His ways and begin to change hearts. He will begin to work with conditions and circumstances regarding your child or teen's life *even* before you learn His Word. As you learn of Him God will be faithful to do His part and preserve and keep your family, (Acts 16:31 KJV; 2 Timothy 2:13; 2 Thessalonians 3:3).

He will show you how to meet the need of each of your children, show you their strengths, weaknesses and their concerns as He places them on your heart. He will begin to give you ideas, guidance, and send people (laborers) across your path that will be a blessing to you and your children in the very area you need it.

Key Points Regarding Adult Children

- **When the parent is assisting their adult child** with finances and/or other support, as their parent(s) they have a right to speak to them about their lives or current situations. The adult child in honoring their father and mother will listen and consider the advice. *However, because the child is now an adult they have the choice of making their own decisions.* The Word of God says, "*Children, obey* your parents in the Lord, for this is right. '*Honor your father and mother,*' which is the first commandment with promise: '*that it may be well with you and you may live long on the earth.*'" Eph. 6:1-3 NKJV and Ex. 20:12.

Adult children are to honor and show respect but as mentioned they make their own decisions.

- **When the adult child asks for their parent's advice** when they are living at home, or on their own or are now married, parents have a right to answer. Although when the adult child is married the couple should go to God first and their spouse second to try to work things out between them before seeking counsel from the outside with Extended Family members or someone else.

- **When the parent is their adult child's employer** or in some other delegated authority position not related to home, once again the parent has a right to communicate to the adult child with work related comments or instructions to secure proper work ethics or to bring a project to completion.

- **The Bible shows rights were given to a grown adult's parents** under certain circumstance. In the Old Testament a newly married daughter who was shamed by the lies of her husband was *vindicated by her father and mother* and if her husband was found guilty the elders of that city would fine him and give the money to her father and her husband was whipped for charging her with shameful things, Deut. 22:13-19.

- **As a mentor or spiritual leader in your adult child's life** you are in a position to judge their spiritual life the same as any other person in your congregation and/or you mentor. When a person calls themselves a Christian then as a spiritual leader it is your responsibility to confront the person caught up in a wayward lifestyle and judge it, I Co. 5:12-13. This is done in order to prevent their blindness (2 Cor. 4:4) from trapping them into an eternal life of damnation and losing the benefit of living in the Kingdom of God while they are still here on this earth, Galatians 5:19-21. *Hebrews 13:17says* **"Obey your spiritual leaders and submit to them** *[continually recognizing their authority over you], for they are constantly keeping watch over your souls and guarding your spiritual welfare,* as men who will have to render an account [of their trust]. [Do your part to] let them do this with gladness and not with sighing and groaning, for that would not be profitable to you either]." The spiritual leader can pray for them and point out they are being deceived and misled! Evil companionships corrupt and deprave good manners and morals and character I Co. 15:33.

- **Cultures and societies may change but God's Word never changes** just as He never changes. *What brought a blessing into your life hundreds of years ago will still bring a blessing today* and what brought a curse hundreds of years ago will still bring a curse today.

Your adult children are a gift to you and at the same time they belong to God. He anointed them, gifted them and chose them to work for Him in His kingdom. Whatever their divine purpose is because of your prayers and the prayers of the saints, yokes will be broken and they will find their way. God will reveal Himself and show them the way. Whatever work He began in them He will continue developing it and finish, Philippians 1:6. At the appointed time they will fulfill their assignment and purpose.

If you as a parent have trained your child up the way they should go then as they are adults, God has a lot to work with. They have enough in them to draw on that will cause them to make sound decisions. In any event the "Breakthrough" (Jesus) will deliver.

The Lord would have you not to worry about your adult children. Worry is in the same family as fear. Living in fear does not please God. It shows a total lack of trust in Him to do only what He can do. It will not move the hand of God. You must set the right atmosphere for God to move on your behalf.

Lift up a praise, say word confessions (read the scriptures you need a breakthrough in out loud).

Worry on the other hand will cause hopelessness and a desire to give up. It can also cause sickness, steal your faith, peace of mind and wear you out. Satan will bring out all his trappings to cause you to miss God and not gain victory. On the other hand, if you *decide to stop worrying,* start trusting and believing your faith will increase and you will be strengthened. In our weakness God is able and willing to make us strong.

Make a decision you will forgive, love them, acknowledge them, receive them and continue to pray for them. Let go and let God all the way. As long as they have one foot with God for safety and one foot in the world their relationship with you will clash and be up and down. It is time for them to step-up and stop being lukewarm and become sold out to Christ. Only the Holy Spirit can do this so it is time for we parents to step back, see about our own assignments as we continue with God. Continue to live our lives as God deals with our adult children and brings them into what He promised He has for them.

The Lord does not distinguish between the different types of families whether it is a Biological, Blended, Single-Parent, Adopted, Foster-Parent, Immediate or Extended Family. In His Word He simply says to all children, humble yourself enough to honor your parent(s) by listening to their advice so your life may be long on this earth.

Children at any age are called by God to honor and show respect to their parents. He did not say if the parents were perfect or the best parents anyone could have asked for. *He said to honor your parents because they are in an office God set-up, anointed them for, placed them in and one He allowed.*

God did not send evil works but whatever the devil meant for harm God will turn it around for good, Gen. 50:20. If things were not *perfect* when the adult child was growing up then they are *also called to forgive and pray for their parents.* In doing so they will be set free from past hurts as God heals their heart.

When they are young He asks us to train them up in the way they should go but **once they are grown continue to love them and allow the Holy Spirit to lead and teach them as He works in their lives.** If they find life is hard or a trial is before them, you can assist as you are requested.

However, after having done all, move aside by placing them and their situation in the hands of God and watch Him move on their behalf. *He said move out of the way because He doesn't need our help to change and heal their hearts, to give them understanding, peace and direction.* He said trust Him with them so we could have a peace as we exercise our faith which will please Him and allow Him to bless us and our household.

Assisting Our Immediate and Extended Family as well as Widows, Orphans, the Elderly and Divine Friends

Providing for Relatives is Discussed in I Timothy 5:8,

> If anyone fails to provide for his relatives, and especially for those of his own family, he has disowned the faith [by failing to accompany it with fruits] and is worse than an unbeliever [who performs his obligation in these matters].

In Regard to Widows and the Elderly, I Timothy 5:1-4 says,

> Do not sharply censure or rebuke *an older man,* but entreat and plead with him as [you would with] a father. Treat *younger men* like brothers; [Treat] *older women* like mothers [and] *younger women* like sisters, in all purity. [Always] treat with great consideration and give aid to those who are *truly widowed* (solitary and without support). *But if a widow has children or grandchildren,* see to it that these are first made to understand that it is their religious duty [to defray their natural obligation to those] at home, and make return to their parents or grandparents

[for all their care by contributing to their maintenance], for this is acceptable in the sight of God. (Emphasis added.)

Isaiah 58:7 Refers to Others that Need Our Help,

Is it not to divide your bread with the hungry and bring the homeless poor into your house -- when you see the naked, that you cover him, and that you hide not yourself from [the needs of] your *own* flesh and blood? (Emphasis added.)

These passages it tells us we are commanded to not only help the needy (widows and the elderly) but not to forget to help our Immediate Family or our Extended Family members and people in the Kingdom of God who are in God's Family and are our spiritual relatives who may also be in need.

Adult Children and adult grandchildren are to attend to their parents and grandparents with material financial support in addition to other areas of support for the care they received while growing up and as a part of showing them honor and respect.

The Lord did not indicate whether this depended upon your parents being the best parents or grandparents, because whatever we do it should be done unto God first. This is a part of keeping God and His ways first and keeping you in His will and under His protection with great favor and for your obedience He will reward you.

Parents like others fall short in many areas this is why we do not look to *people* to fulfill us, return what they took from us or could not give to us in the first place because they did not have it in them to give. Therefore, the answer is simple, we look to the One Who is capable of being all things to all those that choose to receive Him.

A single mother with children in many cases has the same status as a widow with children if she has no support from her former spouse. She is to be given the same consideration and help. *"If any believing woman or believing man has [relatives or persons in the household who are] widows, let him relieve them..."* I Timothy 5:16. A household can include Extended Family members.

When people know God is your source and is the reason you are blessed, it will point them to Him and not to you. It is important to give Him all the glory! Maintain a relationship with God so people will truly know Who is able and willing to empower them to be blessed or assist in a time of crisis. They would have learned to go to Him first in their time of need just as you did.

Isaiah 58:8 is What God Does Once Verse Seven is Fulfilled,

> Then shall your light break forth like the morning, and your healing (your restoration and the power of a new life) shall spring forth speedily; your

righteousness (your rightness, your justice, and your right relationship with God) shall go before you [conducting you to peace and prosperity], and the glory of the Lord shall be your rear guard.

We are commanded to help others before we can expect the glorious presence of God to come and continue to bless us. We can expect to receive peace and prosperity for doing what God asks us to do. **His prosperity is designed to make us whole**. It brings provision as well as abundance; a peace of mind; healings in all areas of your life: physical healing, mental healing, emotional healing, financial healing in the form of increase; safety; joy and happiness. It also brings good relationships into your life; restoration and miracles. His abundance includes more than enough and above the ordinary. His wholeness includes nothing broken, nothing missing, spiritually, physically nor financially.

When to Assist Extended Family

Your Immediate Family is the core your Extended Family extends from. The Immediate Family is comprised of your spouse, your children and yourself. An extension to your Immediate Family would be your children's spouses and your grandchildren.

The Extended Family is extended from both the father and mother and includes other relatives related by blood or marriage: parents, siblings, grandparents, great grandparents, uncles, aunts, cousins and in-laws.

The further down the generational bloodline you go the bloodline is not a great thread to cause harm to children born of couples who are related. In about ninety-eight percent of cases fourth and fifth cousins can legally marry.

Assist each as directed in your heart by Holy Spirit. If you do not have clear direction then the Extended Family's needs are attended to after the Immediate Family's needs are met. Do for others as unto the Lord. It may be necessary to draw boundaries and do not allow anyone to take advantage of your time and resources. However, pray and help as you can.

Concerning In-Laws

In-laws are a part of your Extended Family. Extended Family members may or may not be blood related. In-laws are the parents, siblings, and other relatives of yours or your child's spouse. They may have come into the family with different values, morals and so on. Many families work together without numerous in-law problems. However, studies show in-law problems are one of the largest causes of strife in marriages and the family in general.

Part of this is the fault of the couple who has not learned how to cleave to their spouse and is still going to their parent(s) for constant advice and/or assistance for certain things. Many times, this is done without discussing it first with their spouse and can cause conflict in the marriage. (See the *God's Way and Marriage* for information regarding cleaving and becoming one.)

When there is a problem and both sets of parents are involved this may not be good for the entire family. Hardships, hurt feelings and misunderstandings will more than likely be the result especially if one or both spouses are discussing private issues. That could be embarrassing for their spouse and should really stay within their own household for them to work out or decide together to seek outside help.

Otherwise they place their parents in the middle. Now if the couple decides to forgive and both have gotten past it but their parents and siblings have not because of information about their relative's spouse may make things uncomfortable for everyone.

On another note, in many cases in-laws like to offer advice and some sort of material assistance to newlyweds as they are excited and want the best for them. In-laws should realize the adult child and their spouse will need to make their own decisions even if they offer their suggestions to them.

The couple is not to dishonor or disrespect their parents in anyway but realize they must tactfully suggest to their parents they relinquish their responsibility to them while they bring their spouse into position as the two of them are learning to become one.

The married couple needs to remember to speak well of their spouse and not complain to their parents. After all you do not want your parents at odds with your spouse and run the risk of them losing respect for your them. There is always something good that can be said about most people so choose to say something nice or nothing about them at all. (I am not speaking about abusive situations, of course the abused party should speak to someone they feel they can trust).

Honor your in-laws and try to work out any differences in the family using godly principles. Other in-laws such as sisters, brothers, uncles, aunts and cousins could add to the family in a wonderful way. *It could be an exciting time for the children growing up with family gatherings for birthdays, holidays and major events,* if everyone makes a conscious effort to do their part. Pray more instead of interfering, gossiping and being a robber of peace. Life is too short for strife. Jesus/Yeshua said, "...I came that they may have *and* enjoy life, and have it in abundance (to the full, till it overflows) John 10:10.

Divine Friendships Within and Outside of Family

Many divine friendships also occur within the family. "Friendship is a close, intimate relationship in which affection can be expressed freely. The heart of such friendship is the willingness even to give one's life for a friend. Families can develop friendship within the established role relationships of husband-wife, parent-child just as Jesus and His disciples became friends even though He never ceased being Lord" [1] John 15:13-15.

Even though there are divine friendships within a family unit there are also those outside of it. Therefore, help when possible to take care of the concerns of those divine friendships of people outside of your immediate or extended family you know were placed in your life by God. Even knowing certain people were sent into your life continue with prayer, wisdom and caution to keep everything in order and in balance.

The Lord will also place people across your path for you to share or minister to that may not have been intended for a long term divine friendship. Though, we are called to assist them with their needs from time to time or vice versa.

There are reasons we emphasize divine friendships. Over the years we discovered not everyone in your life was sent by the Heavenly Father. There are two ways people come into your life or across your path: (1) They are sent by God or (2) They are sent by Satan on assignment. We do not believe anything is just by "accident." While on your journey certain people will come and go that were destined to be in your life for a purpose and a season.

God blesses us through each other so do not think it strange Satan would choose to curse your life or try to hinder you through others that work for him. Therefore, discern whether someone is in your life because God sent them or if they have ulterior motives that will work against you when given the opportunity.

Discern and pray about the people that come into your life. God will instruct you as to those to help and/or fellowship with. He will also give you a gift of discernment for those that are there merely to drain you and pull on the anointing, amongst other things I Cor. 12:10. You will want to avoid weariness, becoming burned out, irritable, or feeling like you are about to lose your mind. We are on the right track for maintaining a right mindset and receiving sound instructions for each day of our lives when God is kept in the forefront.

As we realize a part of God's plan is taking care of the family He has entrusted and blessed us with. *He has set in place an order to help it run smoothly.* We should also realize if we are out of order in any area this will eventually cause the family to fall apart through no fault of the Lords but our own. His Word says, "Apart from Me you can do nothing," John 15:5.

God is no respecter of persons, as our family members adjust to His will and timing over a period of time we will be able to see positive changes, growth, experience joy and peace. On the other hand, if our family members do not adjust and are not willing to work with the guidelines and teachings in the Holy Bible then they will experience unnecessary pain, suffering, disappointments, division and failure.

I Peter 3:17 says,

> For [it is] better to suffer [unjustly] for doing right, if that should be God's will, than to suffer [justly] for doing wrong.

Whether we are with God or not, all people suffer to some degree in this world about something because we live in a fallen world where there is *good and evil*. It was not God's will, nor did He ordain mankind should suffer but once man fell (Adam had a free will to make choices) evil was released through the sin of disobedience: death, sickness, poverty, pain, curses, torment, suffering and so forth came upon the earth, Genesis 3.

However, with the right choice of receiving the Savior, you can be redeemed and start a new life and watch things turnaround for your good and the good of your loved ones.

Chapter 8
Opposition Toward Family
from Different Parts of Society

Opposition against the family is very real! Most of all, the opposition that stands against the family, its real objective is to stop the advancement of the Kingdom of God. The persecution and attacks are destined to become worse unless what the Bible refers to as the "True Family" rises up and takes its rightful place in all of the earth.

As it was explained in chapter two, who and what the "True Family" is, know they will rise up in this hour and take a stand against persecution and the opposition is coming from all sides. They will be used to preserve what God has promised and given to enhance life, to promote wellbeing and wholeness. (Discussed further on in the chapter).

Therefore, receive in this time of harvest: joy, freedom, liberty, prosperity and love for each and every family.

The family (which includes the institution of marriage) is the key foundation as well as one of the components or institutions that help form and shape society. *It is currently being attacked on all sides along with other institutions that help govern and shape society and the cultures within it.* The other institutions or "Seven Mountains," as they are referred to are, religion/faith; education;

government/law; business/economy; media/news; and the arts and entertainment industries. They have all been heavily affected and as a result are in disarray and dysfunction.

These mountains, which shape and form society have all been attacked with heavy persecution, slander, chaos and evil practices of all kinds. The sin that entered into the world after the fall of mankind is currently being magnified because of the time and season we live in, known as the End-Times or the Last Days. Note – this is not the end of the world but the end of an age as we know it, 2 Timothy 3:1-9; Matthew 24:1-44 and Daniel 12:1-2, 4.

Unfortunately, because of these attacks both spiritually and in the natural against the family's very foundation, these subtle attacks have been consistently chipping away at its moral fiber. This has been occurring since the fall of mankind. However, since the Industrial Revolution from about 1820, which included the invention of the train, airplanes and the way society functioned in general the moral fiber of society has been attacked to a much greater extent.

With the creation of Israel as a nation, as prophesied in the Bible, and coupled with the signs Jesus Christ gave regarding the end of the age this generation would not pass away. In the last forty years to the present, evil has become much more apparent. Basic things like joy, peace, good relationships, abundance, homes, resources, and so on have been withheld and made extremely difficult to acquire for the average family. (See *The Tri-Tribulation Rapture of the Church* by Dr. Robert L. Dickey for information and revelation regarding the times we presently live in.)

There is always the exception but the norm shows even if the physical needs are met for the family household the emotional and spiritual needs are usually lacking. What should have been wonderful memories of one's childhood with their family, once grown are instead painful, stressful and sad memories for many adults.

So many have been robbed of their childhoods and quite frankly aren't doing much better as adults. Many adults are still acquiring a string of regrets and wishing things were different. *Things will only change and the negative cycle will only stop when they decide to do something different in order to make it cease!*

Even though the attacks (financial problems, poverty and heavy debt, rebellious children, divorce, foreclosure, illnesses, betrayal and so forth) continue on a large scale on families, individual households do not have to experience these attacks in such a way that they do any real harm or damage. The Bible says, "A thousand may fall at your side, and ten thousand at your right hand, but it shall not come near you" Psalm 91:7, just choose to believe it.

Thank God He always gives "His own" a way of escape and He will never allow more to come on someone than they can bear. Since many of you have been robbed in the area of a wholesome family the Lord has provided for many of you a new family and a fresh start with a "True Family" just waiting for you at your command. I am not speaking about acquiring a brand new physical family (even though for some that will happen) but *I am speaking about your current family coming alive and being brand new.* This may sound crazy to the natural mind but not to those who can believe.

When you join God's Family you will begin to sense and feel something has truly changed. Many will receive an immediate breakthrough, miracles, peace and joy with this change. But for most it may not happen overnight, there may even be challenges in the beginning as you adjust, grow and mature into your new lifestyle. *However, one thing is for sure,* once everything comes full circle you will find you are no longer living with regrets but with hope in a future you probably never thought would happen for you.

As we choose to trust Him at His Word He "is able [to carry out His purpose and] do superabundantly, far over and above all that we [dare] ask or think [infinitely beyond our highest prayers, desires, thoughts, hopes, or dreams] to Him be the glory…" Ephesians 3:20.

Some Marriages and Families are Opposed more than Others by a Spiritual Enemy

This leads me to my next point. *Some marriages and families have a better chance at living a fulfilled life than others even though there is great opposition from a spiritual enemy.*

Let's begin with a Traditional Nuclear Family (a middle-class biological family) which functions differently and is different from a Family of God. Although they may look and seem very similar the difference is still there and very real. Many of the foundational standards, qualities, values and guidelines a Traditional Nuclear Family has comes from the Bible. This is one reason they seem similar.

However, *the Traditional Nuclear Family's values are primarily formed from man's thoughts.* Furthermore, conclusions were drawn from the exposure families had to television programs spanning from the fifties and sixties to the seventies and eighties, thereby making the "Traditional Nuclear Family" the primary role model used to describe what a family is *supposed* to be and as a result of this, all other types of families are compared to it and fell short.

Nevertheless, in the time we now find ourselves living, ***the spirit of anti-Christ is already on the earth.*** This spirit is about bondage, captivity, evil and destruction. *The family is a high priority and targeted for destruction. Primarily because it is the foundation and backbone of society and the fact Satan hates people and who they are to God.*

He especially hates those who know who they are in Christ! Therefore, those existing on traditions and men's opinions will find it will not be enough to defeat the evil that is upon their families in this hour.

However, those who do know who they are in Christ and live as mature Christians will have access to the authority given to them in the *Name* that is above every name. They will also have access to spiritual gifts and a host of angelic beings to fight alongside them during this spiritual warfare battle. They fight from a position of victory and will win the war as long as they don't give up and maintain relationship with the True and Living God.

Co-Habiting and Different Types of Unions that Oppose and Threaten Our Society

The terms Co-Habiting or Non-Traditional Families are used in some texts to give the impression people who choose to simply live together have now become a family. This is not biblical and they are not a family that has been sanctioned or approved by God even though God loves them, He will not go against His Word.

Therefore, they are roommates, friends who share a dwelling and they can certainly do the things families do but *they are not recognized as a family in the eyes of God nor anywhere by the laws of the land. They are not a Spiritual Family either because a Spiritual Family takes heed (pays attention) to the teachings of the Lord.*

There are forms in place in certain States for couples who choose to co-habit or live together to receive special privileges and benefits as if they were a family unit, such as medical and dental coverage and as a beneficiary on an insurance policy.

Also, "Common Law" is applied and practiced in certain States to protect an individual's rights, but none of these documents in and of themselves constitute (establish) or fall under the definition of what a "family" is. Be mindful whatever God declares and does it is always for our good. This is where faith and trust come in, *you may not understand His ways but it would be wise to trust Him at His Word because of Who He is,* Psalm 24:8, 10; Rev. 1:5-6; Rev. 3:7; Isaiah 53; Luke 5:5.

Secular schools and universities basically teach young people there has been a change in the nature of the family. There has been a shift from an agricultural society to an industrial one that weakened or gradually and secretly removed many of the family's traditional functions. They say many of the functions of the family are now handled by schools, hospitals, government agencies, peers and hired help mainly because now the family purchases goods and services rather than producing or providing them itself.

Notice how many different resources they speculate it would take to replace the *"family"* as if it were even possible. *They are also taught the family is no longer a necessity but rather it is simply one of many choices they have.*

In addition, to the schools and universities the media also encourages adolescents and young adults to forego marriage and instead co-habit. This is considered by some the main alternative for marriage, stating it is faster, easier and without a strong commitment of any kind. *Their instructions indirectly give permission to live outside of the Judeo-Christian biblical guidelines which were set in place by God Himself for the protection of people through marriage and family life.*

They took it upon themselves to teach a way of life that will lead students astray and leave them empty. God has not changed, He is the same yesterday, today and forever, Hebrew 13:8. He will continue to love us and lead us by His Holy Spirit if we continue to seek Him for truth and the abundant life He promises to those who will seek and receive Him as their own.

In some cases, the influence from the sixties and seventies where people who were fed up with the Traditional Nuclear Family because it seemed to not be going anywhere. Therefore, **some decided to experiment with open marriages, communal living, trial marriages of living together** of which all sounded appealing. *Later it was discovered over a thirty-five-year period that the result of these experimental relationships were empty of value and meaning.*

People were misplaced within the unit of the household (they did not understand their role or function) and strong family units overall were not formed. As a result of this, today many young people are afraid of being a part of a meaningful relationship with real commitment. They may desire it, but they also fear it, because they do not know what a committed relationship really is. Again, for a lack of role models and what the Traditional Nuclear Family had to offer or were accomplishing raised questions like, what is its true purpose or destination?

With a lack of commitment, which these types of relationships were about, people raised in them learned to be afraid of commitment, the marital contract, and even the marriage covenant because they did not believe it could work. Nor do they believe there is anything to it or the people who raised them would not have fought so hard to make a permanent impression that marriage and a godly family is not the way to go.

God's purposes were ignored and training up a child in the Word of God was not the focus, Proverbs 22:6. This would have *instilled purpose, hope and faith in their future.* Instead, a great number of Non-Traditional Families lost the true meaning of their existence and as a result lost their way.

When these types of unions form, in actuality their reason for their lifestyle being outside of the marital covenant ends up fighting against "marriage." They are not just fighting against a lifestyle of living in a traditional setting, but *they end up coming against the very core and height of what a relationship should and can be.*

They also are participating in a *lifestyle of sexual immorality* which is sin and many dwell in that state for years. As we know "the wages which sin pays is death," if not repented of, Romans 6:23. It could bring death to your spiritual relationship with God and/or a physical death. I might add, all people sin and fall short of the glory of God, Romans 3:23. The answer for recovery is the same for all, receive salvation if you are not saved and repent (have a change of mind and turn from your sin). If not, they will never really find out what they are depriving themselves of in relationship to what God had for them. *They did not realize God only gives the best and He does everything with excellence and for their good!*

He created and formed marriage. If we wait on Him and marry the person He sends and operate within the marriage according to His plan, then we can experience the joy, peace, love and wholeness that comes with the marriage covenant which is the foundation of the family.

Continuing in our discussion of different types of unions we will touch on *families that are formed by consanguineous marriages.* These marriages are between people who are blood related, descended from the same ancestor, especially first and second cousins or brothers and sisters which are forbidden by God, Leviticus 18:6-22.

The chances of children coming into the world deformed because of blood ties being so close is a risk factor that doesn't need to be. Certain families especially of royalty practiced these types of marriages often to keep the royal blood and resources within the royal family. And other well-to-do families for similar reasons are taking the risk of their grandchildren being deformed at birth.

However, fourth or fifth generation of relatives marrying is less likely to produce such an outcome.

Replacement Theology a Device of the Opposition to Cause Division

One of the devices Satan used to cause division between the Church and Jews was Replacement Theology. An erroneous teaching which misinformed Christians and resulted in some Christians (or in some cases those who were Christians in name only) mistreating Jewish people.

This teaching was especially done during the Dark Ages when common people had to rely on the leadership, of the Roman government's approval for teaching that went forth. At that time the leadership was under orders to teach the lie, God was done with the Jews and the Church was to replace them.

Yet, the truth of the matter is, the Bible says Christians are "adopted" into the family of God, Ephesians 1:5; Romans 8:15; Psalm 27:10 and are "grafted" into the family according to Romans 11:17-19. **Therefore, they *joined* the Family of God.** *They were not saved to replace the Jewish people who are God's Family but instead to stand with them in these troubling times.*

"No New Testament author suggested in any way that the Hebrew Scriptures were obsolete, and neither did Y'shua. Y'shua is quoted in Jn. 10:16 as saying, But I also have sheep which are not from this sheepfold: and it is necessary for Me to lead those and they will hear My voice, and they will become one flock, one shepherd. Y'shua was speaking to the Jewish people referring to the heathens as the other flock. In Matt. 5:18 Y'shua said that not one yod or vav would drop from Torah until the sky and the earth would pass away," The One New Man Bible page 1761. (Yod and Vav are the two smallest letters in the Hebrew alphabet. This would also refer to a 'little hook' (dots or curves that the scribes added to identifying certain Hebrew letters.))

To further make this point, the following is an illustration of a family which has children and chooses to adopt other children. Do the adopted children *replace* the natural children? Of course not, the adopted children are a welcomed addition into the family. Even if the adopted child(ren) came *first,* once a child is born into the family the natural biological child should not replace the adopted child. On the contrary, they have the opportunity of becoming one big happy family! Ephesians 2:14-20.

Jewish people are forerunners that went through the *storm* so we Christians would know what to do by their examples of faith, success and failure. If they were perfect there would not have been anything to write about. Furthermore, I don't know of any perfect Christians either, but I do know *all people in the world need a Savior, whether they are a Jew or a Gentile.*

In this hour there is still a plot to destroy the descendants of Abraham's Seed. "Anti-Semitism is still the longest-held and deepest hatred in human history. This animosity had its beginning in the garden when God promised Eve one of her descendants would crush the enemy's head (see Gen. 3:15). The weight of this man-hatred later centered in Abraham and his descendants. God's call to Abraham has been a mixed blessing.

Under God's supernatural protection, the Jewish people have survived, but they have had to endure the wrath of the nations. Since the time of Abraham's call, Satan has targeted this family for extinction. If he could destroy Abraham's descendants, he would thwart the purposes of God in bringing the world's Deliverer through Israel's promised Son." [1]

"Become aware that the world's news media is prejudiced against God's work and God's people," Jews and Christians. "Only those who are God-followers can properly assess history, politics and government. Everything in human history, every current event, is moving forward in His timing. We, therefore, will listen to news with greater discernment, always asking ourselves such questions as, "What is the real story behind this report? What is the Lord doing? How am I to be praying here? Is He expecting me to respond?" [2]

Therefore, as all of us move forward, we need to discern, be alert, awake and watchful of the enemy's devices and tactics. Continue to trust God and receive His instructions through His people who have been sent as forerunners to warn and prepare to keep the peace as much as possible.

Remember, as we side with God we walk in His authority. That authority is for our nation and for our homes and families as the enemy of God is on the prowl to destroy whatever God loves.

We can bless God and help His chosen people which will ultimately affect all people in the world. Choose this day to align with Father God and *say a prayer for the Peace of Jerusalem!*

Pray for the Peace of Jerusalem, Psalm 122:6 - 7,

"Pray for the peace of Jerusalem! May they prosper who love you [the Holy City]! May peace be within your walls and prosperity within your palaces!"

Prayer:

I pray for the PEACE (Sar Shalom – the Prince of Peace) of Jerusalem! May they prosper who love thee (Yeshua). Peace (wholeness) be within thy walls, *and* prosperity (security, safety and wealth) within thy palaces. I receive prosperity because of my love for Yeshua. And I pray for God's completion, God's purposes to be fulfilled for the land and the people of Israel. For my brethren and companions' sakes, I will now say, Peace (Shalom) *be* within thee, all the people of the land. I will also continue to pray for supernatural protection over the nation of Israel and for the Second Coming of Messiah. You are my King and my God

Who favored them to gain possession of the land and Who decrees victories for Jacob/Israel, Psalm 44:3, 4. I further proclaim that Israel shall be saved by the Lord with an everlasting salvation... Isaiah 45:17.

John 14:27 says, "Peace I leave with you; My [own] peace I now give *and* bequeath to you. Not as the world gives do I give to you. Do not let your hearts be troubled, neither let them be afraid. [Stop allowing yourselves to be agitated and disturbed; and do not permit yourselves to be fearful and intimidated and cowardly and unsettled.]

How Do We Take the *Family* Back from the Enemy?

To begin the process, families will need to become aware they have an enemy determined to destroy them. This enemy works through people, systems and institutions on the earth and through demonic spirit beings. They will also need to realize they cannot fight this spiritual force alone. Many of them will begin to receive the revelation they will need a Greater Spirit to fight with and for them.

This will lead many of them to Salvation (receiving a Savior) and join the Family of God. They will learn of Him, His love for them and the promises in His Word are theirs. They will also be trained in spiritual warfare. As they are graced with the authority and power of Messiah Jesus they will begin to do their part in the Kingdom of God.

As families walk up right before God and stand strong, the kingdom of darkness will be heavily affected as heads of families, husbands with their wives at their side both turn to Jesus Christ the Anointed One. He, Who is the High Priest of all Believer's homes will begin to impart instructions, strength, spiritual gifts and strategies to fight evil in this new church age. As these families become a part of the army of God.

As part of God's army in the earth, they are trained to fight back by keeping their priorities straight, fight with the word of God, fight in the spirit through prayer and with obedience to God's Word. As a result, the Kingdom of God will advance and move forward in full authority and power given to them to trample on the enemy.

"We are not wrestling with flesh and blood [contending only with physical opponents], but against the despotisms, against the powers, against [the master spirits who are] the world rulers of this present darkness, against the spirit forces of wickedness in the heavenly (supernatural) sphere," Ephesians 6:12.

But we have been given all authority as man and woman, husband and wife to take dominion back from the enemy of life itself, Genesis 1:26-28. This includes taking back their family and the society in which it belongs. This territory was given to them not to their enemy who deceived and stole it. Jesus came and paid the price and took it back. It is up to us to believe it and operate in the authority given to us.

We Have Been Given the Authority, Luke 10:19

> Behold! I have given you authority *and* power to trample upon serpents and scorpions, and [physical and mental strength and ability] over all the power that the enemy [possesses]; and nothing shall in any way harm you.

As the Kingdom of God through the "True Family" expands and advances it will annihilate, simply demolish evil plots and plans. God's Spirit will be poured out and His perfect will for the family will be totally restored. If the children of the Most High do not step up and move forward the enemy will continue to do havoc and more lives and families will be destroyed.

The Lord gave us the authority and the power to fight for our families. As a covering placed in position by Almighty God, we have jurisdiction over our children's lives. We can exercise spiritual authority.

We are going to take a stand and pray in the understanding (our natural language) and in our spiritual language and put on the whole armor of God. Then receive and follow Holy Spirit's instructions. Demons and principalities cannot and will not prevail, I Corinthians 14:2, 4, 13, 14, 15; Ephesians 6:12-18.

As we the families of God step into our rightful place, knowing our true identity, we will rise up as the Glorious Church/Ecclesia, Jesus/Yeshua, is returning for. We are to be yielded to Holy Spirit and resisting evil devices, James 4:7. We will watch the enemy flee from our homes, cities and countries. We will watch this take place for us, our loved ones, friends and for those in the Kingdom of God.

The Lord says, He is coming swiftly with a new anointing that will destroy yokes and restore the plan and purpose He placed in the earth for the family the beginning. Therefore, the anointing will overtake and overpower the devices of the enemy, the wicked one. God's people will move forward with the fruit and gifts of Holy Spirit, the anointing power of God and take back what was stolen.

Acts 2:17-18 Describes the "True Family" that will Move Forward with Power in the Last Days,

And it shall come to pass in the last days, God declares, that I will pour out of My Spirit upon all mankind, and your sons and daughters shall prophesy [telling forth the divine counsels] and your young men shall see visions (divinely granted appearances), and your old men shall dream [divinely suggested dreams. Yes, and on My menservants also and on

> My maidservants in those days I will pour out of My Spirit, and they shall prophesy [telling forth the divine counsels and predicting future events pertaining especially to God's kingdom].

Please note, Joel prophesied about the "Last Days" anointing, and it was quoted by Peter in the book of Acts. This passage covers male and female, young and old and it is a picture of an Immediate and Extended Family of God ministering in the power of Holy Spirit with the anointing of God. They are moving in the gifts of the Spirit (I Cor. 12:7-11) and others will be operating in the Fivefold ministry gifts found in Eph. 4:11-16; I Cor. 12:28. As they go forth exercising the fruit of the Spirit of love all of the fruit will be released that is listed in Gal. 5:22-23.

When the Family of God is retrained and using its God-given authority, power and angelic forces to help, not only can it take back the family but it will also be instrumental and a great influence in the taking back of the Seven Mountains we spoke about earlier.

This message is a message of hope and one that is attainable against all odds. When God is for you who can stand against you? Romans 8:31. The Bible says, "What is impossible with men is *possible with God,*" Luke 18:27.

Those of a secular/worldly (non-Christian) mindset will only think this information is foolish (I Corinthians 2:14). I assure you, once salvation takes place and blind eyes are opened clarity will begin to be imparted by a loving God to His people. They will be victorious when they follow His ways of righteousness along with His instructions and strategies.

Let us do what He says and we will have what He promised. For instance, when we have His peace, His shalom we will have it all! Shalom is Hebrew and it means wholeness, completeness, contentment, safety, health, well-being, prosperity, success and peace in our covenant. In other words, the result is, nothing broken and nothing missing having a peace of mind and true joy, Isaiah 26:3.

All He asks is we believe, John 6:28-29. As we seek first His Kingdom and His righteousness all these things will be given to us as well, Matthew 6:33. God will do what only He can do and He will bring our families and us into what was purposed for each and every one of our lives. Remember, we are more than conquerors who gain a surpassing victory through Him Who loved us, Romans 8:37.

See *God's Way and Spiritual Warfare* for further enlightenment on this subject. Learn how to speak from a place of victory and expect to win in every battle.

Chapter 9
How the Media Influences the Family

The Influence Through Family Television Programs

Going back for a moment let's look at how specific *family* programs on television affected society. I would like to add, many of the television programs had a significant influence in shaping many of our ideas, values and beliefs about how a family would relate to one another. These influences were carried out within the household, with neighborhood, to how its members functioned in the work place, in the educational system and in society at large.

The media is an extremely strong and powerful visual tool that can influence for better or worse. Know and guard what you see and hear especially on the television, the internet and various forms of media because it will make a difference in your soul and the soul of your child(ren). But most of all it will make a difference in how you perceive information and what you receive into your heart (your spirit) and how you process this information.

Prime time television programs such as Leave It to Beaver, Father Knows Best, and The Donna Reed Show to The Brady Bunch and The Huxtables greatly helped to shape the idea of what the Traditional and Blended Families in America were.[1]

By the same token, many have rejected it over the years because it didn't seem real, it seemed to many, unattainable goals or there was some kind of an imbalance in the way it was presented for everyday life. *Although these shows were for entertainment we have to question the mindset formed because of their influence.*

When these sitcoms and others on their order presented a problem, it was usually solved through humor within a thirty-minute span of time and the families never dealt with any serious issues regarding finances, divorce, in-law problems or serious illnesses just to name a few; these and other important topics that affect many families were never presented as an issue.

Many television programs, which were extremely funny in one aspect but taught many women the only way to obtain what they wanted in a marital relationship was to manipulate, lie, play games and to deceive their spouse in a roundabout way. This was considered alright because it seemed innocent and it was for entertainment purposes. As a result, some young women may think if a husband is to make all the decisions and they cannot ever have their way or their opinion or suggestions never have any place or real value then they would rather remain single before they resort to all the tactics of the character they just viewed. Or even worse, they make a decision to marry and put the practices they learned from television or the internet into operation.

The truth is, the Lord has given a wife to be a help meet. She has the divine wisdom God has given her to enable and help her husband. Therefore, she has to be heard by her husband in order for him to receive the gifts God placed on the inside of her for their marriage, the upkeep of their home, raising their children and accomplishing their dreams and visions.

Therefore, television like so many other media resources portray everything except what is *Biblically written.* There should be programs that would truly entertain as well as give depth and truth that would help relationships instead of harm them. One reason this happens is because the adversary affects the air waves because the people of God don't take dominion over it as it is released on this earth. God gave us dominion but it doesn't do us any good if we do not know how to exercise our authority Gen. 1:26.

There is one older film that comes to mind that was successful in capturing some of the reality that is involved with a Blended Family probably because it was based on a true story. That movie is, *Yours, Mine and Ours*, staring Lucille Ball and Henry Fonda. At the time I first watched this film I was a part of a Traditional Nuclear Family (Biological), married with two young children. Little did I imagine one day I would be functioning in a Blended Family as I viewed on the screen.

The movie was somewhat of a comfort and a model for me after I became a part of a blended family. At the time I had no other reference to draw the experience from nor any books to read in depth on the subject. Neither was I able to locate anything with a biblical perspective on the subject.

This is why it is important to really guard what you watch and listen to. The industry needs to take more responsibility in the hiring of those they entrust to write stories for families. Programs should not be written without any in-depth research or experience and/or receiving from the *One* (God) who has all the answers, especially on this subject.

Things that were expected of couples and families were expectations that were based on the opinions of a room full of writers primarily sharing their own views, opinions, backgrounds, experiences, education and lifestyle as opposed to people writing with an understanding of what was written. Things should have been written from reliable research about marriage and the family. The bottom-line is this, whatever is not based on Truth "God's Word" will eventually be exposed and fall.

Therefore, today we have a worse situation, the opinions of most writers giving their views, opinions, background, experiences, education and lifestyle to the public is the same process but its contents are even further from the truth. I would say based on the billboard ads I see while driving or some commercials during sports events I watch with my husband from time to time (we now fast forward through the commercials or mute them) ***there is an*** *assignment in operation to carry people away from what a marriage, a family or a meaningful relationship could ever be.*

I have also noticed from the type of material portrayed on the air and in the theatres much of it is being written by people who are hurting, who come from broken and very hurtful childhoods and do not seem to have a clue as to what a marriage or family is, how it should function or what its true purpose is.

It appears evident many of the secular writers have no connection to truth or reality; therefore, they have no foundation to work from except their own bad experiences and the demonic forces that have influenced their lives.

The argument to justify their position would be boring unrealistic family lifestyle programs do not "sell" and make money *so they give the people exciting programs full of lies, gossip, sex, sin and bloody murders.* The public according to this minority group of people in the industry probably think the majority of the public like and appreciate their work or they simply have been deceived or maybe they just do not care what the public thinks.

On the contrary most people crave decent and wholesome programs specially to watch with their family. Surveys have been conducted that show the majority of Americans do believe in God and are hungry for good clean entertainment.

Most people know right from wrong but they have become so accustom to nonsense that what is wrong seems right and what is right is now seen as outdated, boring, bias, hateful and wrong. This is the result of the influence from only a portion of media because not all media personnel participate in the attempted destruction of society as we know it.

However, there are decent programs and movies out there as well by anointed writers, producers, directors, actors and a host of behind the scenes people. For the sake of our young families we have to search them out on Christian sites and from other advertisements because their work is not boring and outdated and will help reset healthy family entertainment.

Going back through some of the history that formed the ideas of what a family should be and how it should function, we notice unlike true Biblical values or roles, *the Traditional Nuclear Family accepted values, ways and roles that harmed people in the long run* because of major flaws that were hidden within its institution.

For instance, *television role models regarding marriage and the family gave somewhat of a distorted view to what God originally intended.* In some of the programs during the fifties and sixties there were a number of absentee fathers, devalued mothers and tolerance on both parts from couples who exist for the sake of acquiring this dream life without any input or mention of the One who does the Blessing.

What do we mean by this, the appearance was wholesome with loving homes that were perfect and stress-free, there were almost never any financial struggles, arguing or major disagreements. The family's appearance, especially the mothers, was always perfect, as well as the children's manners. The family seems to survive quite well without extended family (which can be a great support system especially when a young family has small children).

They usually had a neighbor who would pop in from time to time, for the most part. By the way and all schedules worked beautifully each and every day. With little to no mention of God or the church leading one to assume they could always do all things in their own strength. And we know that is simply not true.

Although during this era, it certainly was not as much "drama" or stress is in the culture and daily life as it is now. At the same time, it was not as "calm" for all families because we have *always had an adversary that came against the family.* His tactics during those days were subtler because evil stood out and righteousness was the norm, therefore, evil could easily be recognized.

The enemy of mankind and families has many devices to destroy. These devices are not always recognizable simply because unlike years ago where righteousness prevailed in society, now it stands out and is easily identified. While on the other hand evil is now the norm and it seems to be everywhere, and because of deception and evil devices, it is not easily identified. *Nowadays we must discern by Holy Spirit and receive wisdom, direction, favor, spiritual gifts and much more to live safely and fulfill our purpose,* I Cor. 12:10.

Early Sitcoms and the Male Image

During the fifties and sixties even though there was more of a peace in general in the atmosphere, there was an undercurrent of plots of destruction taking place. Seeds were being planted that manifested slowly but surely. Today we are experiencing the results of those subtle movements of compromising and living lives were based on lies and not on truth.

In addition, we are now seeing and experiencing the fruit of a number of events such as prayer being taken out of schools and certain negative legislation and bills being passed over the years which brought corruption into society.

To further my point the Traditional Nuclear Family was not flawless and did set trends that later during the eighties had to be processed and dealt with.

Another hidden reality from television programs was the importance of the male in the home in the programs regarding a Traditional Nuclear Family. The father either worked long hours that kept him out of the home on business trips, or overnight in the city to avoid the long drive to the suburb and so forth.

When he was home he was either in his study, or with his neighbor. On occasion he would be with the children, usually only to correct or instruct or having conversations with his wife discussing decisions that needed immediate addressing for the household or children.

When he was physically present, usually he was emotionally somewhere else, very much detached. No one complained because he was the "bread winner" who was expected to supply this great life for his family. The problem, however, was the father's absence created an irreplaceable void in the home. *He was encouraged and allowed to love his family by neglecting them in order to earn a living to achieve a career and financial success.*

This detachment was devastating. Why? The father's presence is extremely important to validate and affirm his wife and children. *He is the source and sustainer, the head, the protector, the teacher, the primary one that disciplines, he is a nurturer, and he is the very foundation of his family.*

When a father speaks his voice usually commands a certain amount of respect and not out of fear but a reverence for his position in the family. This position was given to him by God and we are to respect God's order. *This man's wife was never intended to replace him but to help him in his functions and endeavors* to achieve the desired results and goals set-up by God for him in his primary role as a *family* man and elsewhere.

Needless to say, the father in today's television program is portrayed as an idiot in most shows if he even exists at all. This is a spiritual attack on the structure and order for the family that was set up by God. Also notice most of the children in some of these programs know more than their fathers.

Furthermore, the man who for whatever reason could not earn a living (not shown on the television programs till the eighties), the pressure of no income was difficult and embarrassing as seen in programs such as "Good Times." In this particular program the father stayed with his family but was unsuccessful in securing work to properly take care of them.

The program was so negative and really exploited the African-American male to the point where the lead actor complained and the studio's response was to eventually write the father figure out of the script altogether and the television series' wife and children carried on without him as if he were never present. This created even a more negative role model for the African-American family.

Sitcoms and Negative Family Images

During the sixties the welfare system began and some programs were modeled after the system. I discovered from observation, many men were unemployed and unable to marry or take care of their children so women with small children applied for state assistance.

For those in the *system* who were married and fathers, they were indirectly informed they could not live in the same home with their wife or marry their girlfriend in order for her to receive state/federal funds. This system was pretty much written into television programs in the eighties to exploit certain people groups even though any person from any people group could apply and receive assistance.

These poor role models were portrayed in the media and sent a negative image. Since neither the man nor woman was employed funds from state/federal assisted living was the only income for their family.

Therefore, men were trained to stay away so these funds could take care of the family's basic needs. Many people from all walks of life, backgrounds and races become entangled with this system in their youth usually because of teen-age pregnancies.

One additional thing, this system whether from watching others from their generational bloodline or watching on television programs encourage women to have children out of wedlock in order to secure funds and be able to be a stay at-home mom.

In essence this system opposes marriage and family life. This is a system of bondage, one that strips people of their dignity and decision making. The sooner anyone is able to leave it and pursue employment which is given by God, the better their life will be.

If someone is receiving state/federal aid I suggest you change your perspective and see it only as a stepping stone while you train for work. Pray and ask God for your purpose and what it is He would have you to do. He will surely answer you if you *really* desire to know, Matthew 7:7; Jeremiah 29:11.

As you begin to receive instructions in your heart about your purpose or goals begin to write them down, Hab. 2:2-3. Also, you may be led to enroll in some type of trade, college, apprenticeship program, or start a business. Who knows, there are so many options and if you have the grace, wisdom and favor of God *nothing is impossible.*

Likewise, in some of the early sitcoms such as the Ozzie and Harriet Show the husband and neighbors were at home all the time and never went to work. Neither did the program ever explain how they acquired an income because the wife was a stay-at-home mom or what is known today as a homemaker. These men maintained homes, vehicles, furnishings, had children but no one worked. If he were an absentee owner, a proprietor of a business I do not recall it ever being discussed or his making a trip to the business or seeing any employees all the years it aired.

This was another negative image primarily because it sent a message that you can have "things and the American dream" with little or no effort. So young people see this and think they are entitled without work, study, trade, qualifications and so forth. They demand things without resources and expect it to materialize. When they cannot acquire as hoped some become angry, selfish, demanding, depressed and hopelessness has an opportunity to set in and cause other problems.

Yes, a destructive plot was in the making that was larger than any human system. There is an enemy that is fighting to keep the man out of the home and to destroy the lives of his children.

Without a father role model many sons never experience the presence of a father in a way that helps him to learn what it means to be a whole man. One who is secure with himself. One who is happy to be a man. Who has a healthy and proper perspective about what a man is and his responsibilities as a husband, provider and father.

Even though it was the early programs that contributed to start the ball rolling using media to bring depreciation of the family structure from where it was to where it is now. The so-called current family programs not only attack the father figure as head of his family but they teach young people to disrespect both parents.

They are being taught to reject authority in the home and in the society in which they live. This is another tactic of Satan. He too rebelled against his authority when he was the most beautiful angel with the most responsibility of all the archangels. He became jealous of Almighty God and decided he would make himself *like* the Most High God.

As it is told he ascended to heaven from the earth where he was living and ruling at the time to exalt himself and was instead met by the archangel, Michael, and was thrown out of heaven with a third of the angels who came with him and who had already been deceived by him, Isaiah 14:12-16.

If our young people continue watching these distorted programs they will set their lives up for much more confusion, frustration, pain and grief because *no good thing can come out of anything that fights the very plan of God.* That is the same as fighting God Himself and He said, "He who is not with Me is against Me, and he who does not gather with Me scatters abroad" Matt. 12:30. But the Word also says, "If God is for us, who [can be] against us? Romans 8:31. It would be better to be on the winning side, which is God's side!

Early Sitcoms and the Female Image

There were a couple of distortions regarding women in these early programs that were hidden and now we are seeing the outburst from women as a result. Women were devalued in the Traditional Nuclear Family. Her primary and in most cases *only* role was to support her husband in his career and to raise her children. There is nothing wrong with that, it is a part of her function if she is a wife and mother.

However, when her value and identity were measured *only* with reference to her husband and children never in terms of herself as an individual with self-worth, goals, desires or dreams, she increasingly became a person with no identity.

During this era, the media portrayed her as a person who was unsupported, isolated and considered unimportant by the world's standard and many times bored with the same routine. *We understand that God desires that a wife's highest priority is her family and her home but is that her only priority?* Except for the fulfillment that she was a good wife and mother, which is highly commended especially for the strengthening of the family in any society.

This is enough for some women but is it enough for every woman? (This was addressed in Chapter Six, however, here we are making a comparison of how this role was portrayed in the media.)

The Traditional Nuclear Family introduced into our society, undue imbalance and suppression of women. Some women felt there was a need to "rebel" against an unjust world that placed so many limitations on their self-worth and choices".

Bottom line, the wives were limited and/or devalued and the husbands were distracted from what was really important. "The true examples and uniqueness of both of these roles were distorted and neglected in the media. Both the husband and wife in the roles of the Traditional Nuclear Family's priorities were distorted simply because people that wrote the scripts wrote their own cultural values into the structure of the family rather than looking at God's Word (the standard that we should live by) Who originally designed and formed it to succeed" [2] Paraphrased.

Because the Traditional Nuclear Family was based on the writer's own experiences and cultural values it did not benefit the family at large in a real society. *We all could have benefited from seeing a strong foundation and/or support system to build from. Also, the satisfaction of knowing we were accomplishing something that would bear good fruit and would last for generations to come.* This would have been believable and received as well instead of just focusing on one household that affected one generation which in and of itself displayed no roots or foundation and possibly very little future.

Sometimes people think we are making too much out of a simple television program. My response would be, just look around at society and then ask yourself what is one of the most profound influences in people's lives? Regardless of what is said or read, *the media is the second greatest influence in our lives coming in second only to watching and listening to what our parents say and do.*

It is the strongest influence with watcher day in and day out. It is the primary example before them as their children grow up. Children learn about marriage the same way. Is it no wonder with all the pressure on families that children witness growing up and once an adult they decide to remain single?

Whether they see the Traditional Nuclear Family obtainable or not, it is seen as a hopeless situation to most. Because some will obtain "the dream" and find even those that have acquired the "good life" are still empty inside. Others may see it as something that is too far to reach or believe for because of their background and where they are starting from and they will not even try to obtain it.

What is not realized is any lifestyle will be hopeless without the Hope Giver. Without faith and strong beliefs in "Someone" that is real and can fill any void in one's life, many are discouraged and give up. The confirmation of this is that the programming of that era and even now is extremely void of any reference to God and/or church in their scripts except on occasion using extremely religious denominations.

The media in all forms and capacities, especially the internet that is currently working to depreciate marriages with pornography, luring teens into sex trafficking and illicit relationships. Not to mention all the different types of shams and robberies directed at homes and the list goes on. In all fairness the internet can be used for good as well and it does connect people all over the world.

Again, if we would heed (pay attention) to the advice of a Wise Savior who said, guard what you see, hear, and say wherever you go, this simple advice would save lives and certainly assist in saving the family structure.

Both parents are very important in God's design. The father and mother carry different responsibilities. When coupled with the Word of God as the foundation for their principles and actions within their home they will be able to function with confidence and assurance as they form and develop well rounded and balanced human beings.

Even though there were problems with the Traditional Nuclear Family many of the children grew up and were very successful and basically had normal lives. Every type of family has its problems and out of them there will be those who succeed in life regardless of the flaws.

Still the issues with some of the children that grew up in a Traditional Nuclear Family and how they themselves felt the injustice of this imperfect arrangement and how their decisions affect our lives today will be addressed as well.

Many from that era tried to find alternatives for themselves. Some of those alternatives included open marriages, communal living, trial marriages of living together. Which only leads us to where we are today with more people living together and higher divorce rates.

Even though many of these couples did eventually marry after possibly years of living together still many divorced later. After living together and then marrying most do not realize there will be a major change after their marriage vows are spoken because now they have become one in the spirit supernaturally. In addition, God is now a part of the union through the marriage covenant.

They will need to become one as a married couple and acquire like-thinking as they come in agreement with issues, challenges, changes, family, work and all concerning daily life. Their goal should be to strive to function as a team once married. (See *God's Way and Marriage* for details on becoming one.)

Issues with Children, Teens and Adolescents When Role Models are Outside of Your Home

Many young children and teens are growing up entirely too quickly and as a result are missing their childhood not only because of wrong choices being made in some of their homes by their parents and/or guardians but because our society tends to bridge preteens, teens and young adults in the same category. Different influences in the life of our pre-teens and teens come from role models outside of the home through the mass media which has a great influence.

The television, internet, smart phones, magazines, music, videos and other electronics introduce a whole new lifestyle to children that are too young and immature to handle. A lifestyle which brings confusion, guilt, shame, pain and hurt because they are trying to comprehend information they are not ready to process and are not prepared to be something they are not called to be and should not become.

One of the greatest influences is their apparel. Adolescents are dressing more like pop stars for everyday life and losing their own identity and gaining attention in areas that are negative and, in many instances, dangerous.

Furthermore, it is difficult to shop for pre-teens and teenagers because the fashion industry does not and will not recognize pre-teens and teenagers are not adults. They are very impressionable and under a great deal of pressure to be accepted from their peers. Therefore, the fashion industry capitalizes on this and uses it as an opportunity to increase their sales. [3]

The parent's responsibility is to have raised a child in a holy atmosphere so when they do come of age and are making more decisions for themselves it will be a little easier on everyone because the child would have learned what is right or wrong, and what is appropriate and inappropriate.

However, if you are a parent who did not bring your child up in the Word of God and now they are rebelling, will not listen to you and they have no fear of authority of any kind including the reverential fear of God, you must take a stand. Let it be known what type of lifestyle and dress is acceptable and not acceptable in your house.

First, you should shop with them or if that isn't something you are able to do or wish to do, then more than likely you will give the money to the teen to shop for clothing and accessories. But make it clear what type of clothing articles are acceptable and are to be purchased. Send someone to go with them if possible. Hold to your standard and don't compromise because you will compromise your child's standards as well.

Second, when they step out of your front door into the public's eye let them know you are interested in how they dress, that they represent the family and if they are a Christian they represent God. It is not so much you care about what people think (although you should not want people to think the worse because of the appearance of how your child is dressed) but more so you and your teen should be concerned about what does God think and what kind of message are you sending. They should desire to be people of excellence pleasing to God and a good example for those younger than they.

Chapter 10
The Benefits of Being a
Family of God

When God is the head of a *family* that places that family in the category of a Family of God, a biblical and spiritual family, *because they have been set apart (sanctified/holy, special) for His purpose.*

Psalms 128:1-6 is a Description of a God-fearing Family,

BLESSED (HAPPY, fortunate, to be envied) is everyone who fears, reveres, *and* worships the Lord, who walks in His ways *and* lives according to His commandments. For you shall eat [the fruit] of the labor of your hands; happy (blessed, fortunate, enviable) shall you be, and it shall be well with you. Your wife shall be like a fruitful vine in the innermost parts of your house; your children shall be like olive plants round about your table. Behold, thus shall the man be blessed who reverently *and* worshipfully fears the Lord. May the Lord bless you out of Zion [His sanctuary], and may you see the prosperity of Jerusalem all the days of your life; Yes, may you see your children's children. Peace be upon Israel! (Also see Psalms 1:1, 2.)

When He was at the door knocking they chose to invite Him in, Revelation 3:20. Once they have invited Him in, some have asked how will their family be different from other families?

The Anointing Makes the Difference

The difference is the "Anointing" that is on these families. They were anointed when they became Children of God through salvation. When they placed Father God, His Word and Holy Spirit first in their lives, even before their own families, the anointing gave them power. That is the order of God and when we are out of order it will hinder and affect the anointing. By keeping Him first He is in position to protect everyone.

The anointing has the power to destroy yokes and cause the new and refreshed to come alive, Isaiah 10:27 NKJV. The anointing is the very presence of God flowing in your life. It will give you the authority and power necessary to accomplish an assignment or your purpose for Almighty God, Psalm 23:5.

The anointing is the power of God on our lives to enable us to do the things God would have us to do we could not do without Him. Things are accomplished by the Spirit of God and not by our might and our power according to Zech. 4:6.

How can the anointing do all of this? Because the anointing comes from the *Anointed One, the Messiah,* Who said, "With men this is impossible, but all things are possible with God," Matthew 19:26. We further find these words in Luke 1:37, *"For with God nothing is ever impossible and no word from God shall be without power or impossible of fulfillment.*

Will the anointing lift or leave you once you are saved? There are many types of anointings and God gives to each what is needed for their destiny to be reached and fulfilled.

The Word of God tells us in, I John 2:27, the Anointing is Permanently with Us,

> "But as for you, the anointing (the sacred appointment, the unction) which you received from Him abides [permanently] in you; ...But just as His anointing teaches you concerning everything and is true and is no falsehood, so you must abide in (live in, never depart from) Him [being rooted in Him, knit to Him], just as [His anointing] has taught you [to do].

Can we hinder or block the anointing from flowing in our lives? Yes, most definitely. Unforgiveness, bitterness, rebellion against delegated authority and other types of sin and evil works will block the anointing and the glory of God from being able to work through you because of your heart issues. God looks at the heart and He is the only Judge of a person's heart.

In order to protect the anointing on your life there are a variety of things that can be done. One is to, "Be submissive to every human institution and authority for the sake of the Lord, whether it be to the emperor as supreme, or to governors as sent by him to bring vengeance (punishment, justice) to those who do wrong and to encourage those who do good service," I Peter 2:13-14.

Submitting (giving respect and honor) with a godly response to *upright* delegated authority (those in authority over you) provides you with spiritual safety. Submission protects us from demonic attacks.

Additional things can be done to protect the anointing is to be obedient to the Word of God, forgive quickly, repent (change your mind and decide to go in the right direction – the way of the Lord). Stay peaceful and calm as much as possible by being slow to anger. Be patient and kind exercising the fruit of the Spirit and so on, Gal. 5:22-23. All of these things work together to protect the anointing God has given to us.

Also realize things are accomplished by the Spirit of God and not by a person's might and power Zech. 4:6. Remember, it is the anointing that qualifies your family, Isaiah 61:1.

What the power of God will do for one family He can and will do for another as long as they acknowledge He is the Anointed One and strive to do things His way.

He will Never Leave You and Always Offers Love and Hope

In this family you are never alone, you are never forsaken or forgotten and is why we may boldly say: "The Lord is my Helper...I will not fear...What can man do to me?" Hebrews 13:6. You will always be loved. Protection, security and provision is available as God meets your needs. All you have to do is ask and if your request is in His will your Father in Heaven will provide it for you His way and in His timing.

His Word says, "Ask, and it will be given to you; seek, and you will find; knock, and it will be opened to you. Everyone who asks receives and he who seeks finds, and to him who knocks it will be opened," Matthew 7:7-8.

Hope is given to all in the Family of God. Even though you are a family within the home *each person who has a personal relationship with the Lord is anointed and entitled to prosper in health, joy, peace, wealth, strength and confidence.*

Knowing who you are in Christ, knowing what your assignment or purpose is, being assured all the promises of God are yours because you are trusting Him daily. In this family there is opportunity to have peace beyond *your* understanding and hope for a great future, John 14:27.

Thus, each person being secure in the knowledge of Christ for themselves sets a great atmosphere in the home. As a result, they will be perceived as a family, an anointed family, a family which was formed by Heavenly Father.

The only way to become a part of and join the family of God, that offers eternal life and outstanding benefits is to receive His only begotten Son, Christ Jesus (Yeshua HaMashiach) as your personal Lord and Savior. Father God (YHVH) will then receive you by adoption.

Ephesians 1:5-6 tells us,

> For He foreordained us (destined us, planned in love for us) to be **adopted** (revealed) as His own children through Jesus Christ, in accordance with the purpose of His will because it pleased Him and was His kind intent]— [so that we might be] to the praise *and* the commendation of His glorious grace (favor and mercy), which He so freely bestowed on us in the Beloved. (Emphasis added.)

John 3:16-17 KJV says,

> For God so loved the world, that He gave His only begotten Son, that whoever believeth in Him should not perish, but have everlasting life. For God sent not His Son into the world to condemn the

world; but that the world through Him might be saved.

As a Family of God, will Our Family Change in the Natural?

We briefly discussed the spiritual change but what about the difference in the natural? **For instance, in the natural,** if they were a Biological or Blended Family they still are; if they were a Single-Parent, a Family by Adoption, Child-Free or a Foster Family they remain so.

This is only an illustration to show the physical structure of your family has not changed but *who they are on the inside has changed because of Who lives inside of them as a result of Salvation.* The change on the inside will soon speak for itself as your family continues in the Lord and study His Word to learn of His will and His ways.

The Family of God, a biblical and spiritual family that keeps God first and is striving to do things His way will experience the following benefits: make better choices because of divine wisdom; forgive others quicker; extend grace to one another; attitudes can quickly change for the better; personalities can flourish and have more inner joy; members of the family will exercise the fruit of the Spirit more readily; understand better how they are supposed to function; learn and know how to take authority over their circumstances; know how to set the atmosphere in their home, to be a pleasant and inviting one; and shake-off demonic attacks and assignments. Recognize distractions and receive wisdom to stay focused as you continue moving forward.

They will also learn to be more considerate in their speech with the right words, tone and attitude towards each other; and most of all be more at peace, have understanding, trust and less insecurity.

In addition, there are four key things that will assure you success in life. With the Spirit of God working through you and you making a decision you want the victory, if you do these four things victory will not have any other choice but to manifest in your life:

(1) Remain committed to that goal you are striving to reach. Especially the one Almighty God said was yours.

(2) Be determined and do not allow setbacks to stop you. Seek God for instructions and strategies. With Him on your side you will have every tool available for victory.

(3) If we choose to wait on the Lord and move forward in His timing all of the correct connections will be in place so we can obtain the prize and bring closure to this endeavor.

(4) Learn to rest in the Lord. Trust and allow Him to show you how to rest in Him. Not worrying, not being frustrated doing a lot of things in your own strength to make things happen. But spiritually and physically resting so you can be refreshed and ready for restoration (the new that is coming to your life).

Additional Benefits

We have a God that loves us with an everlasting, unconditional love. A God we can call Abba - Daddy - and Friend.

A Family of God will also have an opportunity to experience the Higher Life as opposed to the Lower Life as referred to in the book of Matthew chapter ten.

God's grace (unmerited favor) to receive mercy for our mistakes and failures. The provision is already made for you, Hebrew 4:16.

God's Presence (His Spirit) dwells inside of us. His presence is with us always and comes upon us to do a work we could not have done without God's help. In the Old Covenant God's presence was *with* the prophets, kings and the priest and it came upon them to do a work for the Lord. But His Presence, His Spirit did not dwell inside of the people until the New Covenant was effective through Jesus.

God's goal for the Church today will benefit each and every Believer. God is restoring His church. He is calling some to the fivefold offices (apostles, prophets, evangelists, pastors and teachers), Eph. 4:11-16. "His intention was the perfecting *and* the full equipping of the saints... that they should do the work of ministering toward building up Christ's body (the church)." The fivefold offices are to usher in the structure of the

Church Jesus/Yeshua gave to the Early Church to usher in the Kingdom of God. They will operate in the gifts of the Spirit to fulfill this assignment, I Cor. 12:7-11, 28.

As God's glory is released with greater power, the people of God will walk in new levels of healing the sick, creative miracles, giving accurate prophetic words, winning the lost, teaching the Word of God, driving out demons and bringing forth deliverance to set people free. As well as taking back territory stolen by the adversary. This will include the marketplace and the seven mountains.

Generational mantles will be picked up again. These are unique gifts and callings from God. They are being passed down through the generations. For example, in the Old Testament mantles were passed from one person to another as in the case of Elijah to Elisha.

Families did a similar thing, a family passes on their favor, spiritual authority, influence and more through a generational impartation. For example, Abraham to Isaac. These impartations help to maintain the family's spiritual and natural inheritances.

The Word offers protection, stability, blessings, faith, good health, strength, fruit of the Spirit, joy, and a place of refuge. The word of God has whatever you need.

As a child of God, we are called, anointed and appointed by God for greatness and destiny in His Kingdom. As we week Him first we have righteousness, peace and joy in the Holy Spirit.

Holy Spirit is our Teacher, Deliverer, Helper, Advocate, Standby, Strengthener, Intercessor, and Comforter. He is here to have close fellowship with each and every Believer.

We are forgiven for all of our sins and the ones we have yet to commit. The price has already been paid!

David in Psalm 103 NIV Praises the LORD for His Benefits,

Praise the LORD, my soul; all my inmost being, praise His holy name. Praise the LORD, my soul, and forget not all His benefits-- who forgives all your sins and heals all your diseases, who redeems your life from the pit and crowns you with love and compassion, who satisfies your desires with good things so that your youth is renewed like the eagle's. The LORD works righteousness and justice for all the oppressed. He made known His ways to Moses, His deeds to the people of Israel: The LORD is compassionate and gracious, slow to anger, abounding in love. He will not always accuse, nor will He harbor his anger forever; He does not treat us as our sins deserve or repay us according to our iniquities. For as high as the heavens are above the earth, so great is his love for those who fear Him; as far as the east is from the west, so far has he removed our transgressions from us. As a father has compassion on his children, so the LORD has compassion on those who fear him; for he knows how we are formed, he remembers that we are dust. The life of mortals is like grass, they flourish like a flower of the field; the wind blows over it and it is gone, and its place remembers it no more. But from everlasting to everlasting the LORD's love is with those who fear him, and His righteousness with their children's children –with those who keep His covenant and remember to obey His precepts. The LORD has established His throne in heaven, and His kingdom rules over all. Praise the LORD, you His angels, you mighty ones who do His bidding, who obey His Word. Praise the LORD all his heavenly hosts, you His servants who do His will. Praise the LORD, all His works everywhere in His dominion. Praise the LORD, my soul.

Defining a Mantle

In the Old Testament a mantle was a covering. One wore on their body especially if they were a king or prophet. It was used on the body to keep you warm, for protection and to encourage you to rest and have peace. It could also be used for oaths. There were many different kinds of mantles.

Today when you are born-again, we are priests unto God. A physical mantle is not needed. When you learn from a teacher or mentor a mantle is being cast/put on you. A mantle represented a person's gift, the call of God and the purpose for which God has called them. An anointed mantle is a piece of cloth that has been prayed over and unusual miracles took place, Acts 19:11-12.

Defining a Christian

Simply stated, a Christian is someone who has a personal relationship with Father God (YHVH) through Christ Jesus and has access to the power of Holy Spirit by His grace.

A Christian According to The New Webster's Dictionary,

A person who believes in the doctrines of Jesus and acknowledges His divinity and is also a person having the qualities expected of one who professes Christianity.

A Christian According to the Vines Complete Expository Dictionary,

Christianos, "Christian" a word formed after the Roman style, signifying an adherent of Jesus, was first applied to such by the Gentiles and is found in Acts 11:26; 26:28; I Peter 4:16. Though the word rendered **"were called"** * in Acts11:26 might be used of a name adopted by oneself or given by others, the "Christians" do not seem to have adopted it for themselves in the times of the apostles. In I Peter 4:16, the apostle is speaking from the point of view of the persecutor; cf. "as a thief," "as a murderer." Nor is it likely that the appellation was given by Jews. As applied by Gentiles there was no doubt an implication of scorn, as in Agrippa's statement in Acts 26:28. Tacitus, writing near the end of the first century, says, "The vulgar call them Christians. The author or origin of this denomination, Christus, had, in the reign of Tiberius, been executed by the procurator, Pontius Pilate" (Annals xv. 44). *From the second century onward the term was accepted by believers as a title of honor.* (Emphasis added.)

* The word "Call" according to Vines –
Kaleo, derived from the root *kal,* whence
Eng. "call" and "clamor" is used with a
personal object, "to call anyone, invite,
summon," e.g., Matt. 20:8; 25:14; it is
used particularly of the divine call to
partake of the blessings of redemption,
e.g.; Rom. 8:30; I Cor. 1:9; I Thess. 2:12;
and Heb. 9:15.   (Emphasis added.)

In Reference to Being Called, Mark 3:13-15 says,

And He went up on the hillside and
called to Him for Himself those whom
He wanted *and* chose, and they came to
Him. And He appointed twelve to
continue to be with Him, and that He
might send them out to preach [as
apostles or special messengers] And to
have authority *and* power to *heal the sick
and to* drive out demons. (Emphasis
added.)

We are called to God to receive the
Redeemer (Salvation), gifts and a multitude of
benefits and training through study and experience.
Then sent out to minister wherever our assignment
is. Our assignment could be our home,
neighborhood, work place, business and so forth. In
other words, wherever our feet tread and if
someone is in need we are as *Christians called to*

share the Good News of the Gospel and help if we have the resources to do so.

The Meaning of *Children of God* According to The Unger's Bible Dictionary,

The Believer's relationship to God as a child, accordingly, issues from the new birth (John 1:12-13). But all regenerated people are not only children, (that is, born again) but adult sons as well, **children of God receiving a place as sons (Galatians 4:5) by adoption.** The indwelling Spirit (Holy Spirit) gives to the child of God the realization of his sonship or spiritual adulthood (Gal. 4:1-6). Since mankind is fallen, a person becomes a child only by faith in Christ and only members of the *Father's family* are brothers in any vital spiritual sense. (Emphasis added.)

Defining Christianity

Christianity as Defined by The New Webster's Dictionary,

The religion of those who accept Jesus Christ as God incarnate (body, flesh) are guided by the Holy Spirit, and participate in the fellowship of the Christian church.

Christianity came into being 30 A.D. when the Apostles received the power of the Holy Spirit to preach the resurrection and gospel of Christ. *Christianity has molded the shape of Western Civilization and has been carried by missionaries to nearly all the countries of the world.* (Emphasis added.)

Christianity as Defined by The Unger's Bible Dictionary,

The body of doctrine that consists of the teachings and way of life made possible by the death, burial, and resurrection of Christ and the giving of the Holy Spirit. *Christianity although having its roots in Judaism, is not Judaism or a mixture of Judaism. It is a way of life, of salvation, the full expression of the gospel of the grace of God* for this age in which God is visiting the Gentiles and "taking from among [them a people for His name" (Acts 15:14). After this period Christ will return and "rebuild the Tabernacle of David which has fallen" (Acts 15:16). (Emphasis added.)

It is Beneficial to be Joined to the Family God Chose for You

Only God-joined relationships are by divine connection. Being in the relationship with the connection or family God has ordained and doing things His way will bring good results (whether it be a natural or spiritual; many times, both are found in the same family).

As you fellowship with Him, He says ask and He will answer. When He answers it will be His way, in His timing, and it will always be for your good. The results will prosper you in all areas including peace, health, prosperity and wholeness.

However, if you choose to separate yourself from the divine connections set by God without speaking to Him and seeking Him first, receiving confirmation and subsequently connect yourself to someone, for instance in marriage, you could possibly bring a person not sent by God into your life.

This decision could not only ruin your life by robbing you of many precious years and having unnecessary heartache but it will affect the people in your family. Because you decided to have a man-joined relationship instead of a God-joined relationship.

An example of a man-joined relationship would be the story of the prodigal son, Luke 15:15-16. He lost all of his money (his inheritance) and nearly starved to death because of mishandling his inheritance. He later joined himself to a citizen of the country he had traveled to. This citizen sent him into his fields to feed swine. He was so hungry he filled his belly with the husks the swine ate and no man gave him anything.

This young man got into trouble and out of God's will, timing and protection for his life when he left home the wrong way. He disrespected his father by asking for his inheritance early, which was the same as desiring his father was dead so he could receive his inheritance. He left without seeking God first for God's will for his life, direction or protection.

After losing everything he joined himself in a relationship which was not God's will for his life. But when he finally came to himself (having a sound mind, 2 Tim. 1:7) he went back to the family and relationship God had joined him to in his father's house. His father received him back with love, gifts and a celebration.

The lesson here is, if on your own initiative you choose to break loose from someone or a group which God has joined you to, you run the risk of becoming impoverished in more ways than one. But if you make a decision to do things God's way your life will prosper even after you have made major mistakes.

The Bible says in 2 Corinthians 6:14-16,

Do not be unequally yoked together with unbelievers. For what fellowship has righteousness with lawlessness? And what communion has light with darkness?

Thus, a man-joined unit of people have the opportunity to seek God for a turnaround in their life. They can receive salvation, ask for forgiveness and repent for bonding with people God may not have intended for them to be with. This simple act of obedience and faith will give God the opportunity to now make changes and bring restoration into your life. Therefore, wherever changes are necessary God will change hearts, circumstances, situations and so forth so you may experience a better life and a better family.

Always remember, He is our strength, peace, wisdom, righteousness, love and all we will ever need is found in Him!

Scriptures that will Strengthen You as they are Read and Deposited into Your Heart

I have the Greater One living in me; greater is He Who is in me than he who is in the world, I John 4:4

I have the mind of Christ, I Cor. 2:16; Phil. 2:5

I am the temple of Holy Spirit; I am not my own, I Cor. 6:19

I declare My family and I are blessed according to our covenant with God, Gen. 12:3; Gal. 3:8

The Lord has promised salvation for me and my household, Acts 16:31

Blessed shall I be when I come in and blessed shall I be when I go out, Deut. 28:6

I have a God-fearing family that reverently and worshipfully fears the Lord, Psalm 128:1-4

I declare and receive a twofold recompense that I possess double and rejoice in my portion, Isaiah 61:7

I have received the spirit of wisdom and revelation in the knowledge of Jesus, Ephesians 1:17-18

I am a joint heir with Christ, Romans 8:17

My children have authority over Satan, Psalm 127:3-5; Luke 10:19

For it is You Who gives me the power to get wealth, that You may establish Your covenant, Deut. 8:18

My set time for favor on my life is now, Psalm 90:17

Jesus is able to do exceeding abundantly above all that I ask, Eph. 3:20-21

I am strengthened with all might according to His glorious power, Col. 1:11

Christ in me is the hope of Glory, Col. 1:27

God is with me, Matthew 1:23

He promises to be with me, Matthew 28:20

I declare and receive all of the blessings the Lord has granted me, Deut. 28:1-14

It is not I who lives, but Christ lives in me, Gal. 2:20; Psalm 30:1-12

All of my needs are met according to God's riches in Christ Jesus, Phil. 4:19.

Lord show me the way I should go, Psalm 143:8

God blesses me and makes me a blessing to others, Gen. 12:2

I am far from oppression, and fear does not come near me, Isaiah 54:14

I have the peace of God that passes all understanding, Phil. 4:7

I can do all things through Christ Jesus who strengthens me, Phil. 4:13

My children have authority over the enemy. The destroyers in my children's lives have gone, Isaiah 49:17

I am a doer of the Word and blessed in my actions, James 1:22, 25

I am more than a conqueror through Him Who loves me, Romans 8:37

I am forgiven of all my sins and washed in the Blood, Eph. 1:7

I am redeemed from the curse of sin, sickness and poverty, Deut. 28:15-68; Gal. 3:13

The Beatitudes Given by Jesus in Matthew 5:3-11 NKJV,

Blessed *are* the poor in spirit,
For theirs is the kingdom of heaven.

Blessed *are* those who mourn,
For they shall be comforted.

Blessed *are* the meek,
For they shall inherit the earth.

Blessed *are* those who hunger and
thirst for righteousness,
For they shall be filled.

Blessed *are* the merciful,
For they shall obtain mercy.

Blessed *are* the pure in heart,
For they shall see God.

Blessed *are* the peacemakers,
For they shall be called sons of God.

Blessed are those who are persecuted
For righteousness' sake,
For theirs is the kingdom of heaven.

Blessed are you when they revile and
persecute you, and say all kinds evil
against you falsely for My sake.
Rejoice and be exceedingly glad, for
great *is* your reward in heaven, for so
they persecuted the prophets who were
before you.

The Lord is the source of all blessings and we
are called to bless Him through our worship and
faith. We also have the authority to bless one
another.

I pray this writing has been a blessing to you. If your family is not a family of God I pray it will become so and maintain the love, strength, health, power and joy that is offered by the Lord in Jesus' name, Amen.

APPENDIX A

A Prayer for Salvation and the Infilling of the Holy Spirit

If you are not a Born-again Christian with the Infilling (Baptism) of the Holy Spirit, or you are a Christian Believer and would like to rededicate your life to Jesus, say the following prayer. Afterwards, tell someone of the decision you have made regarding the Good News!

Dear Heavenly Father,

I come to You now, just as I am in the name of Jesus. Your Word says, "…Whosoever shall call on the name of the Lord shall be saved," Acts 2:21. And it says, "that if you confess with your mouth the Lord Jesus and believe in your heart that God raised Him from the dead, you will be saved" according to Romans 10:9.

I believe and confess now that Jesus (Yeshua) is the Son of God and He is alive today. I receive Him as my personal Lord and Savior. I ask for forgiveness and repent of my past sins and I choose to forgive others for their trespasses. Thank You Father God that Your Son has set me free from eternal darkness. I now declare that I am redeemed, I am healed, I am blessed, and I am whole. Therefore, I now have a renewed, abundant and confident life in Christ Jesus, the Messiah.

Father God, You said my Salvation would be the result of Your Holy Spirit giving me new birth by coming to live in me Romans 8:9, 11. So I ask You now for the Infilling of Your Holy Spirit as you have promised. Thank You for the gift to speak in other tongues, my spiritual prayer language that is unknown to man but known to God according to Acts 2:4 and I Corinthians 14:2. Now I bind the strong man that was sent to rob me and I plead the Blood of Jesus over my mind and mouth as I now release from my spirit my supernatural prayer language in Jesus' Mighty name. Amen! Give God Thanks!

The above Prayer is based on Romans 10:9-10 NKJV which says,

"That if you confess with your mouth the Lord Jesus and believe in your heart that God has raised Him from the dead, you will be saved. For with the heart one believes unto righteousness, and with the mouth confession is made unto salvation."

I John 2:2, 12 AMP says,

"And He [that same Jesus Himself] is the propitiation (the atoning sacrifice) for our sins, and not for ours alone but also for [the sins of] the whole world. ...*because for His name's sake your sins are forgiven [pardoned through His name and on account of confessing His name]."*

"Justified" – We are as if we never sinned! We are declared righteous, acceptable to God because of the Finished Work at the Cross where Jesus took our sins and gave us His Righteousness because in Him we have redemption through the blood! Hallelujah for a God Who Saves, Ephesians 1:7, Acts 4:12.

Salvation Scriptures,

Romans 10:9-10; John 3:14-17; John 5:24; Acts 2:21; John 10:9-18; John 6:44-51; Ps 51:5; Acts 4:12; Mt. 1:21; I Peter 1:23; Ro. 3:23; I John 1:9; Ro. 6:4; Acts 3:13-26; 2 Cor. 4:4; Eph. 2:8-10; Ro. 5:8; John 14:6; I John 4:9-10; John 3:3-6,15-16; Mt. 12:40; I Cor. 15:22; Acts 10: 40; Acts 16:31; Col. 2:6-7, Acts 15:11

Infilling of the Holy Spirit,

Acts 2:1-4; I Co. 2:4-5; Acts 10:44-48; Acts 1: 5, 8; Acts 2: 39; Acts 11:16; John 4:23-24; Romans 8:6-17, 26-27; John 1:33; Eph. 6:18; Jude 1:20; I Cor. 2:14; I Cor. 6:19-20; I Cor. 14:2-15, 18; Luke 11:13; Ezekiel 11:19; I Cor. 12:7-11; Eph. 5:18; John 16:13; Gal. 5:22-23; Isaiah 11:2-3; Romans 6:1-11

APPENDIX B

What is Salvation?

God so greatly loved the world that He gave His one and only Son, that whoever believes in Him shall not perish but have eternal life, John 3:16. Because of what Jesus did on the cross, a way was made for people (Jew and Gentile) to be reconciled back to Father God through Salvation. This brought forth the "Believer," which is the One New Man, Eph. 2:14-16. "And there is salvation in *and* through no one else, *for there is no other name under heaven given among men by and in which we must be saved,"* Acts 4:12, the Amplified Bible.

In John 3:14-17 Jesus explains,

> And just as Moses lifted up the serpent in the desert [on a pole], so must [so it is necessary that] the Son of Man be lifted up [on the cross], In order that everyone who believes in Him [who cleaves to Him, trusts Him, and relies on Him] *may not perish, but* have eternal life *and* [actually] live forever! For God so greatly loved *and* dearly prized the world that He [even] gave up His only begotten (unique) Son, so that whoever believes in (trusts in, clings to, relies on) Him shall not perish (come to

destruction, be lost) but have eternal (everlasting) life. For God did not send the Son into the world in order to judge (reject, to condemn, to pass sentence on) the world, but that the world might find salvation *and* be made safe *and* sound through Him.

When you receive Yeshua HaMashiach, (Jesus the Christ, the Messiah, the Anointed One) you are saved. "For it is by free grace (God's unmerited favor) that you are saved (delivered from judgment *and* made partakers of Christ's salvation) through [your] faith. And this [salvation] is not of yourselves [of your own doing, it came not through your own striving], but it is the gift of God," Eph. 2:8.

The word "saved" is the English word for the Greek word "Sozo" which was used to define the Hebrew word "Shalom." "To be saved is defined as: to deliver or protect – heal, preserve, save, do well, be (make) whole," (Strong's Concordance).

A personal relationship with God is included. The Holy Spirit is with you, inside of you and will communicate with your spirit. You are also entitled to good health, preservation, protection, provision, prosperity, favor, peace, good relationships, purpose, safety, deliverance, authority, soundness, spiritual gifts, strength, mercy, guidance, angelic help, increase and more! In other words, wholeness (Shalom).

Furthermore, the English word **"save"** is used in the New Testament to define the Hebrew word **"Shalom."** Another term used to describe "save" is **born-again.** Jesus said "unless one is born again, he cannot see the kingdom of God," John 3:1-6; I Peter 1:3.

The name Yeshua (Jesus) means Savior or Salvation. Salvation makes you whole as you grow in Messiah, Matt. 1:21. *Therefore, Yeshua restores "Shalom"* making you whole - nothing broken and nothing missing. He is the Pioneer of your Salvation, Heb. 2:10.

Jesus is also referred to as the Prince of Peace (Sar Shalom) and "Peace comes to you because you are whole!" Hebrews 13:20-21 NKJV says, "Now may the God of peace who brought up our Lord Jesus from the dead, that great Shepherd of the sheep, through the blood of the everlasting covenant, make you complete in every good work to do His will, working in you what is well pleasing in His sight, through Jesus Christ, to whom *be* glory forever and ever. Amen."

To be saved is to have Salvation (Yeshua). Everything you will ever need is found in salvation. *The most important things about receiving salvation is that in Christ you become a new creation; salvation comes with the New*

Covenant and salvation includes eternal life, 2 Cor. 5:17; Jeremiah 31:31-33; Matthew 26:26-29; Luke 22:20; Romans 2:28-29; Galatians 2:16 and Galatians 3:7-14; 26-29; John 3:16, 36.

Salvation prevents anyone from perishing for their sin for eternity in outer darkness. Instead of death they will receive eternal life, John 3:36. In addition, while still on earth the Believer receives "The Blessing" which encompasses all the blessings from the Lord in the Kingdom of God.

Because we accepted the Father's sacrifice, Jesus/Yeshua, the Father *adopted us* into His Family (the Family of God, the One New Man).

Romans 8:15 says,

> For [the Spirit which] you have now received [is] not a spirit of slavery to put you once more in bondage to fear, but you have received the Spirit of adoption [the Spirit producing sonship] in [the bliss of] which we cry, Abba (Father)! Father!

The word adoption basically means a person is brought into the Family of God even though they were previously without any covenant with Him. Like all of us who are born-again (John 3:1-3) we were sinners and separated from God, but God in His mercy and grace redeemed us, purchased us and brought us into His presence. In His presence once again, this time through the blood of His only beloved Son, Jesus.

Once saved we are adopted by God, Who chose and received us as His own. What an honor, for Almighty God to choose us and then pour His love on each and every one of us. As Christian Believers in Christ Messiah, the Anointed One.

We are now eternally part of His family. His Spirit dwells in our spirit man and communes with us. Because of the adoption we become heirs of God and joint heirs with His Son, Jesus the Christ (Yeshua HaMashiach), Romans 8:17.

So how does one receive their salvation? Romans 10:9-10 NKJV, "that if you confess with your mouth the Lord Jesus and believe in your heart that God has raised Him from the dead, you will be saved. For with the heart one believes unto righteousness, and with the mouth confession is made unto salvation."

APPENDIX C

The Father's Blessing Prayer

Now the Lord will bless you and the Lord will keep you and the Lord will make His face to shine upon you, and the Lord will be gracious unto you, and the Lord will give you His peace. And the Lord will make His countenance to shine upon you now and He will establish shalom for you forevermore.

The Lord Himself will go before you and He will send His angels before you to prepare your way and His angels will be behind you to be your rear guard of protection. The Lord will prosper all that you put your hands to. He will make you the head and not the tail. The Lord will give you houses you did not build. The Lord will give you vineyards you did not plant. The Lord will give you wells you did not dig. The Lord will chase your enemies before you because He is the Conqueror of your enemies.

The Lord Himself will be your Counselor. The Lord Himself will be your Healer. The Lord Himself will be your provider in every dimension of your life in your spirit, in your body concerning your health, and in your finances. Therefore, receive this blessing in the name of the Father and the Son and the Holy Spirit.

I further pray that my children as well as my spouse and I truly hear with our spiritual ears the full meaning and receive revelation of what God is saying in His Word. We will grow progressively into maturity as we continue to walk with God as we are led by Holy Spirit each and every day.

(Now add to your prayer anything specific that you would like God to do in the life of your son(s) or daughter(s). This prayer can also include your spiritual children.

Explanation of the *Blessing of the Father Over Your Children*

It is your legal right through God for you and your seed to be blessed! When the spiritual authority of your household (if a single Mom then it is you) releases the blessing, it is something that God Himself honors and therefore the blessing of the father has the ability to sculpture the life of the son or daughter from that moment forward. Furthermore, that blessing cannot be removed, it cannot be changed, and it cannot be broken.

What you say over your child is going to be what God does for your child from this day forward as the blessing releases God's provision, protection and the understanding they are blessed. These prayers will help secure their future. The revelation of being blessed by God because of the finished work at the cross by His Son is the foundation for exposing and defeating the deceiver. Amen.

NOTES

Chapter One:
What is a Family, its Purpose and the Qualities that make it Strong?

1. Disciple's Study Bible, NIV Footnote.
   Nashville: Holman Bible Publisher, 1988
2. ibid

Chapter Two:
The Different Types of Families that Shape and Develop Society

1. Disciple's Study Bible, NIV Footnote.
   Nashville: Holman Bible Publisher, 1988
2. Joyce Meyer, *Hearing from God Each Morning.*
   New York: Faith Words, 2010
3. Disciple's Study Bible, NIV Footnote.
   Nashville: Holman Bible Publisher, 1988

Chapter Four:
God's Order, a Higher Lifestyle, and the Purpose for Family Roles

1. Disciple's Study Bible, NIV Footnote. Nashville:
   Holman Bible Publisher, 1988

Chapter Five:
Biblical Instructions for the Role of the Husband

1. Loren Cunningham, David Joel Hamilton with Janice Rogers, *Why Not Women?* Seattle: YWAM Publishing, 2000.
2. Disciple's Study Bible, NIV Footnote. Nashville: Holman Bible Publisher, 1988
3. A. R. Bernard, *Four Things Women Want from A Man,* New York, NY: Howard Books, 2016

Chapter Six:
Biblical Instructions for the Role of the Wife

1. Loren Cunningham, David Joel Hamilton with Janice Rogers, *Why Not Women?* Seattle: YWAM Publishing, 2000.
2. A. R. Bernard, *Four Things Women Want from A Man,* New York, NY: Howard Books, 2016

Chapter Seven:
Other Family Roles: Child, Adolescents, Adult Child and Extended

1. Disciple's Study Bible, NIV Footnote. Nashville: Holman Bible Publishers, 1988

Chapter Eight:

Opposition toward Family from Different Parts of Society

1. Don Finto, *Your People Shall Be My People.* Ventura, California: Regal Books, 2001
2. ibid

Chapter Nine:
How the Media in Various Forms Influence the Family

1. Robert Lewis and William Hendricks, *Rocking the Roles.* Colorado Springs: NAVPRESS, 1991, 1998
2. ibid
3. John Townsend, *Boundaries with Teens.* Grand Rapids: Zondervan, 1984

About the Author

Audrey L. Dickey, D.Min, Ph.D. is an apostle, prophetic voice, author and conference speaker. She ministers the Word and counsels prophetically to advance the fivefold ministry in the Kingdom of God. Her books include spiritual warfare strategies and tools for marriages, families, finances, everyday life experiences and Kingdom business. Since her youth she has seen signs and wonders, healings and prophecies come to pass through the power of God. Dr. Audrey holds a Doctor of Philosophy in Religious Studies and a Doctor of Ministry with emphasis in Biblical Counseling from FICU in California. She is also a member of the American Association of Christian Counselors (AACC). She along with her husband, Robert L. Dickey, Ph.D. received a vision to establish an international apostolic, prophetic ministry. They are the founders and CEO's of Christian Love Glory International Center as well as the founders and apostles of Christian Love Fellowship Church, Inc. This Fivefold multi-cultural ministry includes covenant restoration of the One New Man and will oversee designated marketplace businesses. Drs. Robert and Audrey Dickey have five children and make their home in Los Angeles, California.

To Contact the Author:
Dr. Audrey L. Dickey
P. O. 48288
Los Angeles, CA 90048
www.robertandaudreydickeyministries.org

Other Books by Audrey L. Dickey

<u>GOD'S WAY SERIES</u>

God's Way and Marriage

God's Way and the Blended Family

God's Way and Finances

God's Way and Knowing the King

God's Way and Divorce

God's Way and Spiritual Warfare

www.ingramcontent.com/pod-product-compliance
Lightning Source LLC
Chambersburg PA
CBHW071950040426
42447CB00009B/1298